MW00679767

Retire Worry Free

Financial Strategies for Tomorrow's Independence

Michael E. Leonetti

Longman Financial Services Publishing
a division of Longman Financial Services Institute, Inc.

Executive Editor: Kathleen A. Welton
Project Editor: Chris Christensen, Ellen Allen
Copy Editor: Patricia Stoll
Design: Edwin Harris

© 1989 by Longman Group USA Inc.

Published by Longman Financial Services Publishing
a division of Longman Financial Services Institute, Inc.

89 90 91 10 9 8 7 6 5 4 3 2 1

Library of Congress Cataloging-in-Publication Data

Leonetti, Michael E.
    Retire worry free : financial strategies for tomorrow's
independence / Michael E. Leonetti.
    Bibliography: p.
    Includes index.
    ISBN 0-88462-107-3
    1. Aged—United States—Finance, Personal.   2. Retirement
income—United States—Planning.   I. Title.
HG179.L445 1988
332.024'01—dc19

                                                        88-8309
                                                          CIP

Acknowledgments

I would like to express my gratitude to all those people who helped shape my theories, and in turn, develop this book.

- To my parents, Michael L. and Delores M. Leonetti, whose continued example of living helped me realize the difference between living and life itself.
- To James D. Schwartz and Harold Gourges, two of the individuals whose theories about financial management and life inspired much of my philosophy.
- To my office staff, whose continued dedication kept my business running smoothly while I took time to complete this work, and without whose assistance the completion of manuscript would have been a difficult task.
- To all my clients, who have allowed me to experience first-hand the trials and tribulations, the ups and downs, the pros and cons, and the good and bad of the times of retirement. My experience in helping these people has allowed me the opportunity to develop the strategies and concepts conveyed in this book.
- And to my wife, Elizabeth, without whose constant patience and understanding this work, and my life's work, would have been a much more difficult task.

Contents

Preface

You are probably trying to find out what type of retirement book this really is. You already may have read through the table of contents and flipped through a few of the pages. You no doubt hope you have found a guide to planning your retirement that addresses the financial concerns that go along with it.

This book is essentially a work of concepts and information. The first part of the book defines retirement in a new light, discusses why you should plan for retirement, and provides you with a methodology for determining your retirement goals and crystallizing the lifestyle of your later years. The second part provides practical information you will need when addressing the financial aspects and strategies of retirement planning. Taking financial inventory, risk management, estate planning, ways to stretch dollars, and investing are all reviewed to present a coordinated approach to planning for your retirement by developing strategies for meeting financial problems and opportunities.

It's never too late, nor too early, to start planning for your retirement. The more time you have to prepare for the possibility of retirement, the more rewarding and comfortable those years can be. There are two factors that make planning ahead particularly important:

- The manner in which you will spend your retirement years in terms of mental and physical activity.
- The financial consideration of how you will be able to maintain your chosen lifestyle.

It is difficult to say which of these factors carries the greater weight. You should not underestimate the critical importance of either one—they overlap and intertwine, and the balance will tip to one side or the other, depending on your individual case. However, your physical and mental health can be profoundly influenced by what you do with your retirement years, and your ability to do what you want may depend totally on your financial resources. The retirement years are a time for continued living and enjoyment, and not a kind of grim holding tank for the grave.

You must plan for this time of your life so that your move into retirement is a comfortable transition from your working years rather than a shock.

This book is also a guide to the understanding of and to the solutions for the financial problems that many elderly people face. By planning for the financial aspects for this time in your life, you can go into retirement with the thought of seeking more enjoyment in your life. Retirement should be a time for all of us to try something new—to get tired all over again.

This book will motivate you to look forward to the retirement years, with a different outlook. Retirement is a time to be adventuresome and to do the things you have always wanted to do.

This book is your map. I hope that you will use this map to avoid the state of uncertainty that many individuals pass through when entering the retirement years. Use this guide to plan for and visualize the life you would like during your retirement years, and go into this time of your life with a full realization that it is a time to enjoy all that life offers.

PART

Setting Your Retirement Goals

1

Why Plan For Retirement?

Psychiatrist Ari Kiev, author of *A Strategy for Daily Living*, has stated that helping people develop personal goals was the most effective way to help them cope with problems. The main reason to plan for retirement is to better cope with existing problems and to prevent additional problems from arising during retirement.

PLAN FOR THE FUTURE. . . TODAY

Although your retirement date may still be many years off, it is never too early to start your preparation for retirement. Most experts agree that the earlier you begin your planning, the better. Yet many people spend more time planning a two-week vacation than they do planning their retirement. Retirement is really a passage from one lifestyle to another. Those who do the right type of planning usually have a smooth trip. Too many people retire to nothing and then wonder why they are unhappy and disenchanted; they never sat down ahead of time to determine what they wanted from retirement. The more you know about what you want, the easier and faster your passage to the retirement years will be.

Without effective planning for this passage, you may find yourself very disappointed with the transition. Most of those who do not plan for retirement find that they are very dissatisfied with what they become, yet reject what they could be by refusing to experience new opportunities afforded them during the retirement years. Planning for this transition and these new challenges allows you to anticipate a new reality. When you quit your job, you lose an identity, so you must create another. Planning for this transition allows you to create that new identity prior to retirement and live it during retirement while phasing out the old identity that came with your job.

Retirement isn't idleness, constant vacations, or slowing down; it is a time in which we can opt for second careers, a totally new lifestyle, and new dreams and objectives. More opportunities are opening up for all ages as retirements and career changes increase. Now is the time to start planning for the future.

Author Peter A. Dickinson, in *The Complete Retirement Planning Book*, prefers to call the retirement years the elective years—indicating that in retirement you can at last choose your way of life rather than having it programmed for you. Advance planning helps you avoid the pitfalls, allows you to realize the options available to you during retirement, and frees you to experience pleasure in your journey to retirement and the life of *your* choice.

The "Graying of America"

According to the magazine *Retirement Living*, a man retiring at 65 can expect to live until he is 81 years old. A woman who retires at 65 can expect to live until 84. Actuarial tables indicate that the odds of a couple reaching a ripe old age together increase with each passing year. According to a report of the United States Senate Special Committee on Aging, less than five percent of the U.S. population was 75 or older in 1982; it is projected that by 2030 almost 10 percent of the population will be in that age group. By 2050, some 12 percent of the entire population is expected to be 75 or older. By the year 2030, it is likely that 21 percent of all Americans will be 65 or older, which will represent a 64 percent increase in a 20-year span.

More than 21 million people in the United States will have turned 65 between 1980 and 1990. Some people opt for retirement at that age; others delay the transition as long as possible. For all, however, the most important question is, "Will I be ready for retirement when the time comes?" Often referred to as "the golden years," the retirement years, without proper planning, can be filled for many with financial worry, boredom, and a difficult adjustment to a new lifestyle. All these factors must be considered while planning ahead to ensure these "golden" times.

Most of us fear the uncertain and the unknown. The best way to conquer this fear and to avoid unnecessary worry is to face the future now. Take time to plan for the future so that retirement becomes a time when you may experience more personal freedom and fulfillment than ever before. A fulfilling and exciting retirement awaits the person who does some thoughtful preplanning. Remember, the key to good retirement planning is to start thinking about tomorrow and planning for it today.

People often postpone planning for retirement because they associate the state of retirement with "old age" and the end of their productive years. Planning for retirement requires a mental adjustment to the prospect of a new life, and the freedom that comes with it.

Do You and Your Spouse Agree?

Differing ideas about retirement are often a source of conflict between spouses because they have never really discussed their preferred lifestyles with each other or even what each expects of the other in retirement. Many couples have only one definite plan for retirement: to take a major trip.

Couples facing retirement need to sit down and talk about their expectations to avoid surprises and to prevent possible disappointment. Spouses should ask each other the following questions:

- What are our plans for daily living?
- Are we going to be together 24 hours a day?
- Are we going to be with each other for the rest of our lives?
- Are we going to move?
- Are we going to travel?

Now more than ever, couples are living longer and retiring earlier. As a result, more and more couples are faced with years of being together all day. For some, this is the fulfillment of a dream. For others it is a nightmare of added responsibilities and increasing irritations. Most of us are concerned about career choices in high school or college, but we rarely think of our retirement path—what we will be doing with the rest of our lives.

Finances.   The subject of finances—what this book is primarily about—can cause tremendous friction, especially when living on the fixed income retirement can bring. Money does not have to be a problem. Some questions couples should ask themselves include these:

- What is the present value of their home?
- How much is their automobile, or automobiles, worth?
- What is their joint annual income from Social Security, pensions, real estate, investments, etc.?
- Do they own stocks and bonds jointly or separately?
- How much life insurance does each carry?
- Who are the beneficiaries?
- Do they have a joint bank account?
- Do they have separate bank accounts?
- Do they have up-to-date wills?
- Do they rent a safe-deposit box?
- Does each know where the key is?

The Let-Down Syndrome

If you plan correctly and early, retirement won't mean retrenchment. You needn't give into the common retirement let-down syndrome. Far too many people retire into a kind of nothingness, lost in their newfound free time and wondering why they feel disenchanted. Take a chance. Don't be afraid to risk your time. Try something totally new; if it is not for you, at least you tried. Forget about the Joneses; you have earned the right to do whatever it is you want to do. Consider a part-time job to keep your mind busy and supplement your income, but make sure the job is something you really enjoy.

The best way to accomplish this is to plan ahead. The more you have thought about your goals, the easier and more pleasant your transition into retirement will be.

What do you want from retirement? Are you financially able to get what you want? How will you spend your time? Set up a financial picture for yourself that answers these questions. The financial aspect of retirement affects all other things. My father once told me you can be an old man or an elderly gentlemen; cash can make the difference. Sad, but often true.

Be Flexible

In terms of your budget, you must know what you are *able* to do. Coordinate your information to form a realistic, workable retirement plan based on facts, and consider all possibilities. Periodically reevaluate your goals and plans, leaving room for changes and course corrections. Be flexible enough to realize that change can and will occur, and remember that your retirement plan should be a guideline, enabling you to change according to circumstances and helping you achieve your objectives.

Retirement planning should allow for the unexpected. It is extremely difficult, if not impossible, to predict the future. Individuals who are supposed to be expert planners have compiled less-than-perfect records. Random, unpredictable events may waylay your plans.

This planning is really better described as organization. Organization will prepare you to take advantage of whatever may come along. Planning for retirement requires that you visualize the lifestyle you would like to lead and review the components of that lifestyle.

What Are Your Alternatives?

Finally, planning involves the predetermination of what your various alternatives are, and the testing of those alternatives before their use is indicated. This planning means not waiting until a decision is immediately upon you, but, rather, knowing what alternatives are open to you ahead of time and about which one you are most enthusiastic. Properly done, this process can be repeated for every financial decision you need to make.

A good example of this type of thinking lies in a recent trip of mine to the golf course where I usually play on the weekends. I usually drive on the same roads to get to the golf course, however I was notified earlier that one of these roads was closed. Knowing this ahead of time, I was able to choose an alternative route and still get to my destination on time. In this manner, I predetermined my alternatives—that is, the roads I needed to take and the time it would require—and then chose the best option to get to my destination.

This way of thinking and planning is what this book promotes. Use this method wisely and often, and you will begin to create the worry-free retirement that you desire.

Above all, you should realize that if you do not plan or create financial strategies for your retirement, you face a potential economic nightmare. Approximately 16 percent of all elderly in the United States live below the poverty level. If they live alone or with persons to whom they are not related, their situation is likely to be much worse. Roughly 50 percent of all these elderly receive incomes less than $3,000 per year, and 83 percent of them receive less than $6,000 per year.

Elderly couples fare somewhat better, yet 20 percent of them still receive less than $4,000 per year, and 75 percent of them receive less than $10,000 per year. Reality for many who are retired means substandard housing or dramatically rising property taxes; eroded purchasing power from Social Security, pensions, savings, and investments; Medicare benefits covering only 60 percent of the total health care costs; and other problems particular to each individual.

In addition, only one out of five men among the elderly is still working, and only one out of 12 women. In 1960, one out of every three men over 65 was working, and in 1950 almost one out of every two. For many, retirement has become a matter of financial survival, eliminating many choices that might otherwise be available during retirement. Rather than being able to choose between going out to eat or playing an extra round of golf, many of our elderly today are faced with the difficult decision of what to do when the money runs out when they simply cannot make it stretch any further.

Planning is critical if you want the opportunity to choose among alternatives that present themselves for your enjoyment during your retirement. You not only *should* plan, you *must*.

2

Determining Your Retirement Goals

When asked what retirement means, many people describe it as the time they stop working for pay. While retirement may mean stopping or reducing the time spent in a job, it should not be associated with an end to anything. Rather, it should be the transition to a different lifestyle—one that you desire and for which you have planned.

WHAT DO YOU WANT?

Ask yourself the following questions:

- Where do I want to be during retirement?
- What do I really want to accomplish?
- If I had to choose tomorrow between two lifestyles, which of my personal goals would most influence my decision?

If you don't have good answers to these questions, chances are you're cheating yourself by wasting some of your own time, effort, and money pursuing things you don't really care much about.

9

This is hardly unusual. In my practice as a personal financial planner, I constantly see intelligent, well-heeled people running like mad to get someplace they really don't want to be. The sad fact is that there are few things people dislike more than planning.

A rare person knows exactly what he or she wants. The value of really knowing what you want cannot be underestimated. Obviously, if you know where you want to go, you're a lot more likely to get there.

Career Fact Find

To help people find out what they really want out of life, Jim Schwartz, a financial planner, developed a process called the Career Fact Find. Through a series of questions and exercises, the Career Fact Find seeks the underlying goals and dreams that form the fabric of each of our lives. The process also helps rank each individual's personal goals so they can be considered in making realistic choices.

The Career Fact Find helps bring back-of-the-mind goals into sharp focus. It can also evoke new ideas to consider in making personal and professional decisions. This method helps in charting the best course for the future.

To give you an example of how the Career Fact Find can work, consider the following: Not too long ago, a very successful lawyer came to Schwartz for financial advice. He had just been through an amicable but painful divorce and needed help rearranging his finances.

Bob McNaulty (not his real name) was a managing partner of one of the top law firms in the state. Descended from a poor family, he had clawed his way to the top, forming and building his own firm and pushing it up. By the time he came to Schwartz, his income topped $100,000 a year, and he was working a ten-hour day.

Through the Career Fact Find, Bob identified several goals, some of which helped alter his course. One of the most apparent of Bob's goals was to be recognized as a success. This he had clearly done through his law practice; however, he had other, conflicting, goals. He had a strong sense of family unity and, with his recent divorce, he feared losing his children. He also had a need to take on challenges, and the challenge had long since gone out of his law practice.

Looking at his goals from the Career Fact Find, Bob realized that by continuing his present course he would certainly lose out on one, and maybe two, of his real wants in life, so he changed course. He handed the management of his firm to another partner, announced he would work only a three- to four-day week at the firm, and decided to devote the rest of his time to keeping in touch with his children and to establishing a legal clinic for the poor. He still had the law firm and, surprising both himself and Schwartz, his income remained about the same.

Schwartz's Career Fact Find files are filled with other similar examples. He recalled a talented young architect torn between two job choices: going with the brand-new, solar energy–oriented firm in town or going with a much older, establishment-type firm. He thought he should go with the new firm, but his Career Fact Find showed a constant striving toward stability and security. As a result, he joined the older, firmly established firm. In another case, a banker left her plush job with a large downtown bank to help start a fledgling suburban bank. Why? She discovered her most important goal was having a good deal of authority, which she knew she would probably never get with the downtown bank.

Personal financial planning is merely a way to achieve life's goals; retirement planning deals with those life goals relating specifically to your retirement. Any good financial/retirement plan must have at its foundation your personal goals. Career Fact Find may help you define these goals.

Preparing for the Goal Fact Find.   Before starting on the Career Fact Find, make sure you have the following at hand: First, you will need two to three uninterrupted hours. (You have thousands of hours ahead of you, so you might as well spend a few hours now planning for them.) Second, you will need a large pad of paper on which to write your answers to the Career Fact Find questions and exercises.

As you work through the question-and-answer portion of the Career Fact Find, keep one rule in mind: *generalizations do not count.* You must be able to back up every answer or statement you make with a specific incident. If you don't, you're wasting your time. For example, you can't say you are proud of becoming independent unless you can back it up with something like, "I stopped writing home for money," or, "I no longer go into fits of paranoia when colleagues don't agree with me."

After you have finished with the question-and-answer portion of the Career Fact Find, you may wish to take a break of several hours or even a day before starting with the goal determination and ranking process. Sometimes this short hiatus will help you remember new facts or incidents to use in your Career Fact Find calculations.

The Career Fact Find.   The question-and-answer portion of the Career Fact Find is divided into six parts: Achievements, Decisions and Turning Points, Complaints, Areas for Improvement, Missions and Dreams, and

Geography and Money. Be sure to answer each question (with the possible exception of Number 25), since the overall pattern of your answers will reveal your true goals.

To help you with these questions, sample answers have been created for each question. However, these answers are general—not as specific as yours should be. (For example: "I can't manage well." In this case, you would perhaps say, "My project is months behind schedule, and two people just quit.") For your own purposes, don't forget you must have a specific instance or example in mind for each answer.

Use the sample answers only as guidelines to the types of answers you should give. If you try to mimic them or stick too closely to them, you'll confuse your final results.

1. What was the most enjoyable evening you had in the last two weeks? Why? (Perhaps your most fun was going dancing because you love hot, noisy bars or maybe you enjoyed staying home reading a book because you don't get much chance to read.)
    Most enjoyable evening: _____

    _____

    Why? _____

    _____

2. What are you most eagerly anticipating in the next two weeks? Why? (A picnic because it will take you into the mountains? A department meeting at work because you'll finally get that new proposal off the ground?)
    Eagerly anticipating in the next two weeks: _____

    _____

    _____

    Why? _____

3. What are you particularly proud of? (This can include business awards, achievements, personal achievements, sports, or whatever. Some people talk about winning golf or tennis tournaments; others talk about promotions or new jobs.)
    Particularly proud of: _____

    _____

4. List three things you have learned to do in the last five years that you couldn't do before. (This can include almost anything—overcoming a fear, gaining a new skill, and so on. For example, learning how to fly without going into near-hysteria or finally discovering how to make your new computer work.)

Learned to do (three things): _____

_____

_____

5. What occasions have you most enjoyed at work? At school? At play or leisure? (Examples: strategy meetings at work, making a new presentation; getting an A on the final exam you should have flunked; breaking 90 on the golf course.)

   Most enjoyed at work: _____

   _____

   At school: _____

   _____

   At play or leisure: _____

   _____

6. In what activities do you get so absorbed that you lose all track of time? (Examples: creative writing, preparing blueprints, or working with very complex calculations.)

   Absorbing activities: _____

   _____

   _____

Decisions and Turning Points.   Next, you need to draw your own lifeline, revealing important times and decisions of your life.

7. A horizontal line is shown below. Segment this line into different ages (10, 15, 20, 25, 30, 35...). Draw vertical lines at the correct chronological age to indicate important decisions and turning points. For example, decisions and turning points may include college, marriage, birth of a child, death of a parent, and choice of a career. But don't limit your decisions and turning points to just these. Be sure to list everything that has had an important impact on your life. Your lifeline might look like this:

Sample Lifeline

Joined Scouts	Bought first car	Took job at bank	Got married	Mindy born	Became full partner

Age:	10	15	20	25	30	35

8. For each decision or turning point, list below it what you think might have happened if you hadn't made that decision or had that turning point. (For example, on the sample lifeline, if you hadn't gone with the bank when you were 22, you might have followed your other interest—and become a mechanic.)

9. On a separate sheet of paper, list your regrets—either the things you wish you had not done to date in your life or the things you wish you had done. (Maybe you wish you had gone ahead and worked toward a higher degree in your field, maybe you wish you hadn't left your hometown, and so on.) Place the most important of these regrets on your lifeline at the correct chronological point.

Regrets: _____

_____

_____

_____

_____

_____

_____

_____

_____

_____

10. Look over your lists of significant achievements. Place the most important of these on your lifeline.

11. Draw a complaint chart as follows. Fill this in with the appropriate answers. (You can list as many complaints as you like.)

I Can't	Specific Instance	Because	If I Am to Change This, I Must...
Make a good presentation	I fell all over myself last Wednesday	I'm afraid of speaking to groups	Join a club, get more practice
Work well with Tim	We haven't spoken for two days	The boss has set us up in too many little competitions	Ask Tim to lunch and try to talk to him about it

I Can't	Specific Instance	Because	If I Am to Change This, I Must...

12. Now repeat this chart, except fill in what complaints others—your boss, friends, family, colleagues, and so on—have about *you*. (For example: Others' Complaints: "My colleagues say I won't accept their input." Specific Instance: "I ignored Harry's advice on the new contract." Because: "I generally like to work by myself." If I Am to Change This, I Must: "Consciously strive to be a team player or get a new job.")

Others' Complaints	Specific Instance	Because	If I Am to Change This, I Must...

13. List your complaints about other people and things—what ticks you off about your job, lifestyle, friends, family, colleagues, and so on. (Examples: you hate having to keep time records at work, you dislike having to get together with your neighbors every Friday evening, Harry drives you crazy with his nit-picking.)
Complaints about others: _____
_____
_____

14. In what areas do you need to improve? (Be specific: "I can't seem to write clear memos." "I keep forgetting to go through my in box." Or, as a nonskill example: "I need to spend more time with my family." "I have to control my temper a little better."
Needed improvements: _____
_____
_____

15. What—in your own estimation—do you consider to be your failures, or the areas in which you have not been successful? List these in order of importance to you and specify why you consider each a failure or nonsuccess. Place any significant failures on your lifeline in its proper chronological order. (Examples: "I failed to get that new contract the company needed." "I flunked out of grad school.")
Nonsuccesses: _____
_____
_____
Why? _____
_____
_____

16. You have just found Aladdin's lamp and can make three wishes—what will they be? (A tennis court outside your house? That your boss's boss will finally catch on to his expense-account games?)
Wish 1: _____
Wish 2: _____
Wish 3: _____

17. What would you do differently if you just received a tax-free gift of $1 million? (Quit your job and take off for Tahiti? Go back to school for your doctorate? Start your own business?)
Would do differently: _____
_____

18. What have you always wanted but never gotten? (A motorcycle? Your very own, private hideaway?)
Always wanted: _____
_____

19. What is the one thing you do that makes others really happy? (Make them laugh, feel secure, or feel important?)
Make others happy: _____
_____
_____

20. If you could make a 60-second prime-time commercial about any issue or belief of importance to you, what would it be about? (Advo-

cate mandatory exercise programs for the entire population? Call for an end to all government regulation on business?)
Your 60-second commercial: _____
_____
_____
_____

21. If you were president and could pass any three bills, what would they be?
Your three bills: _____
_____
_____
_____

22. What are your favorite recurring dreams?
Favorite recurring dreams: _____
_____
_____
_____

23. Assuming you had only one year to live and you didn't want to spend it traveling, what would you do? Why can't you do it now?
I would do: _____
_____
Why not now? _____
_____
_____
_____

It's probably time to get back to money—as in how much money do you really need?

24. To help determine your real money needs, make a chart as shown below. In the "Have to Have" column, fill in the *minimum* amount of money you and your family could live on for a year. (Only consider *necessities* here—don't tell me you "have to" have a club membership!) In the "Ought to Have" column, fill in the amounts of money you think you need to maintain a decent, but not wildly extravagant, lifestyle. (You can add in that club membership here if you really want it.) Finally, in the "Nice to Have" column, fill in all the things you would really like—all the frills you didn't consider in your "Ought to Have" column. Make your best educated guess on the cost of each of these frills, add it all up with your "Ought to Have" living costs, and decide the amount of money that it would be "Nice to Have" each year.

Have to Have	Ought to Have	Nice to Have
Room and board for 3	Health club membership	Vacation home
Medical care	House, not apartment	Country club membership
Transportation to work, etc.	Better car	Sailboat
Basic clothing		

Have to Have	Ought to Have	Nice to Have

25. This question concerns geography. Some people say they simply could not stand to live in certain parts of the United States. If you're one of those people, you'd better add geography into your Career Fact Find. In general terms, write out the description of your ideal— or "must"—place to live. (Example: mountains, seashore, four seasons, or 70 degrees year-round)

"Must" geography: _____

_____

Your answers to the above questions and exercises will help you see the unique fabric of your life. The key now is to find the recurring patterns in that fabric.

Spread out the pages on which you have answered questions 1 through 23 (we'll get to questions 24 and 25 later). Look carefully through all your answers, seeking common threads or themes. What you want to find are the things you frequently work for or against and the common goals that run through your answers.

2 / Determining Your Retirement Goals   19

For example, your answers to the exercises may show that you seek independence (you left home at an early age, you left a job because it felt stifling, or one of your dreams is to make it on your own), or your answers may point toward a need for structured situations. You may show a constant striving toward a particular business or type of activity (the oil business, the arts, or helping people). Your answers may reveal a strong need for individual recognition, a love of team play, or a dislike of routine work.

To get to your true goals, do not rely on the image you've always had of yourself; look at all your answers. And remember, a goal doesn't count unless it is backed up by the empirical evidence of your answers.

Now write down seven to ten goals in terms of retirement lifestyle criteria. These should be no more than one to three words each—for example, independence, stability, becoming an architect, time flexibility, and so on.

List these goals down the side of a page. Now add on your "Ought to Have" items, your "Nice to Have" items, and, if it's important to you, your ideal geography.

Your Goals

_____

_____

_____

_____

_____

These are your goals in the retirement phase of your life. Since you will rarely find a situation in which you can fulfill all goals equally, you now need to rank them for setting your course.

First, look over all your goals and choose the two or three that you consider musts—the things you must have to be happy and fulfilled. This is where you first cut priorities.

Musts

_____

_____

_____

_____

Having removed the "musts" from your list, number the remaining goals (the wants) from 1 to 10, or however many you have. (You should have reduced your list to no more than ten; otherwise, the ranking process will become very awkward.)

Wants

_____

_____

_____

_____

_____

_____

_____

_____

_____

_____

Now rank each of the "wants" so that you will know the relative priority of each. To do this, set up a pyramid as shown in figure 1. Taking the first two lines of the pyramid, you will compare goal 1 with goal 2, then with 3, 4, and so on. The question you should be asking yourself is, "If I had to choose between goal 1 and goal 2, which would I choose?" and continue on down the line. In each case, put a circle around the goal you have chosen. When you have finished with the first two lines, move to the next two lines, comparing goal 2 with 3, 4, 5, and so on.

After you have worked through the entire pyramid, count up the number of times you chose each goal. (In the example pyramid, the individual chose goal 1 four times, goal 2 twice, goal 3 once, and so on.) Write the number of times you chose each goal next to the goal. This is the rank, or priority, you have assigned to that particular want in your personal outlook. Now use the choice matrix to make a decision among several options.

For this choice matrix (which can be used for almost any type of choice), you will assign each "want" goal a score based on its ranking. For example, in the sample pyramid, the individual chose goal 1 four times, so it has a maximum ranking of 40; since he or she chose 2 twice, it has a maximum ranking of 20.

FIGURE 1 Ranking Pyramid

1	1	1	1	1	1	1	1	1
2	3	4	5	6	7	8	9	10
	2	2	2	2	2	2	2	2
	3	4	5	6	7	8	9	10
		3	3	3	3	3	3	3
		4	5	6	7	8	9	10
			4	4	4	4	4	4
			5	6	7	8	9	10
				5	5	5	5	5
				6	7	8	9	10
					6	6	6	6
					7	8	9	10
						7	7	7
						8	9	10
							8	8
							9	10
								9
								10

1 = _____

2 = _____

3 = _____

4 = _____

5 = _____

6 = _____

7 = _____

8 = _____

9 = _____

10 = _____

Now you are ready to work through the matrix. First consider your "musts." Does each option satisfy the listing? If any option does not satisfy an item, immediately strike it from your consideration.

After you have eliminated any option that does not satisfy a listing, you are ready to work through the goals. For each option, ask yourself how likely that option is to satisfy a goal. For example, starting with goal 1, you may decide that option A will totally satisfy that want. Since goal 1's maximum score is 40, you should enter 40 in the column for option A. Now you may decide that option B is only fairly likely to satisfy goal 1; based on your own judgment, you put a score of 30 in the column for op-

FIGURE 2   Sample Ranking Pyramid

1	1	1	1	1	1	1	1	1
2	3	4	5	6	7	8	9	10
	2	2	2	2	2	2	2	2
	3	4	5	6	7	8	9	10
		3	3	3	3	3	3	3
		4	5	6	7	8	9	10
			4	4	4	4	4	4
			5	6	7	8	9	10
				5	5	5	5	5
				6	7	8	9	10
					6	6	6	6
					7	8	9	10
						7	7	7
						8	9	10
							8	8
							9	10
								9
								10

1 = 4
2 = 2
3 = 1
4 = 7
5 = 8
6 = 5
7 = 5
8 = 4
9 = 5
10 = 4

tion B. You may decide that option C is unlikely to satisfy goal 1, so you assign a score of 15, 10, or even 5. You must be the judge.

Continue working through the choice matrix, asking yourself how likely each option is to satisfy each goal and assigning scores based on your own judgment. Remember, you cannot assign a higher score for each goal than the maximum determined from the relative ranking of the goal. (In other words, in the pyramid the individual chose 3 only once, so he or she cannot give it a higher weight than 10.)

FIGURE 3

Goals/Maximum points	Option A	Option B	Option C
Must 1			
Must 2			
Must 3			
Goal 1/			
Goal 2/			
Goal 3/			
Goal 4/			
Goal 5/			
Goal 6/			
Goal 7/			
Goal 8/			
Goal 9/			
Goal 10/			
TOTAL			

When you have completed the entire matrix, add up the scores. The option with the highest total score is most likely to fulfill your personal criteria—and will be the best choice for you!

Now you have a listing of your personal goals, their ranking, and a strategy for using your goals to make some of life's difficult choices. The plans you make for yourself through this process should help you realize both your personal life goals and your specific financial goals.

3

Creating Your Later-Years' Lifestyle

Setting financial priorities is often difficult; however, it is very important since few of us have the financial resources to totally finance all of our wants.

Setting priorities allows a conscious review of our objectives. It also helps separate "must" objectives from "ought-to-haves" or "nice-to-haves," thus encouraging a financial commitment to what is most important. Setting priorities prevents individuals from forsaking their most important long-term objectives for the satisfaction of fulfilling recurring short-term wants.

The Forced-Choice Model

To assist you in clarifying and ranking goals, critical steps in financial planning, a forced-choice model can be used. (This model is useful for helping with almost any type of decision.) Once priorities have been set, you must decide how to achieve those goals. The options are often numerous, and the decision chart will help in that process.

Start writing on a sheet of paper all the things you want in life. Include every want, from something specific, such as a boat, to something more nebulous, such as a comfortable retirement. Number the items. To assist you, here is a sample list:

1. a new car
2. a boat
3. a comfortable retirement
4. funds for the children's education
5. a vacation home
6. sufficient money to leave spouse at death
7. braces for children
8. a hair transplant for husband
9. an entertainment center (without the frills)
10. a dog

Now list these numbers down the side of a different piece of paper.

Work through the forced-choice model in figure 4 and begin making choices. (Refer to figure 5 as an example.) Start with the first two rows, working from left to right; you can see that the choices concern your first objective as compared with all the other objectives. Begin by choosing between satisfying objective 2 or 1, then 3 or 1, and so on. Then move down to rows three and four, which concern objective 2 versus all other objectives. Remember, you must choose one or the other (this is a forced-choice model).

After you have worked through the entire model, count the number of times you chose to satisfy each objective and write this number next to the corresponding figure for that objective in the column to the left of the model.

In figure 5, a high priority was given to leaving the spouse enough money in case of death (objective 6, with nine preferences), and a very low priority was given to the hair transplant (objective 8, with no preferences).

The Decision Chart

It is rare that we are willing to totally give up one objective to satisfy another. Normally, we either partially satisfy both objectives or slightly modify the objectives, either through requantification (for example, saying we want $3,000 per month for retirement, then changing it to $2,500) or substitution (satisfying the new car objective by purchasing a Chevy instead of a Mercedes).

FIGURE 4   Pyramid for Forced-Choice Model

1	1	1	1	1	1	1	1	1
2	3	4	5	6	7	8	9	10
	2	2	2	2	2	2	2	2
	3	4	5	6	7	8	9	10
		3	3	3	3	3	3	3
		4	5	6	7	8	9	10
			4	4	4	4	4	4
			5	6	7	8	9	10
				5	5	5	5	5
				6	7	8	9	10
					6	6	6	6
					7	8	9	10
						7	7	7
						8	9	10
							8	8
							9	10
								9
								10

Objective	No. of times selected
1	_____
2	_____
3	_____
4	_____
5	_____
6	_____
7	_____
8	_____
9	_____
10	_____

A decision chart can help you choose among desirable options. Objectives are listed on the left-hand side of figure 6. Along the top are listed asset allocation options. A weighting factor is listed next to the objectives; this is calculated by taking the total number of objectives and multiplying it by the number of times that objective was chosen as a preference in the forced-choice model. The result is the maximum number of points you are allowed to allocate to this objective relative to its

FIGURE 5   Sample Ranking Pyramid for Forced-Choice Model

Forced choice model

2	3	4	5	6	7	8	9	10
2	(3)	(4)	5	(6)	(7)	8	9	10
(1)	1	1	(1)	1	1	(1)	(1)	(1)
	(3)	(4)	(5)	(6)	(7)	8	(9)	10
	2	2	2	2	2	(2)	2	2
		4	5	(6)	7	8	9	10
		(3)	(3)	3	(3)	(3)	(3)	(3)
			5	(6)	7	8	9	10
			(4)	4	(4)	(4)	(4)	(4)
				(6)	(7)	8	(9)	10
				5	5	(5)	5	(5)
					7	8	9	10
					(6)	(6)	(6)	(6)
						8	9	10
						(7)	(7)	(7)
							(9)	(10)
							8	8
								10
								(9)

Objective	No. of times selected
1	5
2	2
3	8
4	7
5	3
6	9
7	6
8	0
9	4
10	1

being satisfied by each option. In the sample shown in figure 7, ten objectives are listed. Objective 1 was chosen as a preference five times in the sample forced-choice model (figure 5); thus, the maximum points available are 50 (10 × 5). This procedure is continued until the decision chart weighting column is calculated.

From here, it is necessary to determine how well each objective will be served by combinations of asset and cash flow allocations. For instance, if option A is chosen, it may satisfy objective 1 very well, but it

FIGURE 6   Decision Matrix

			Options:			
Objective	Times Chosen	Weight	A	B	C	Etc.
Total						

may hardly satisfy objective 2 at all. Here, one must make a subjective allocation of points available for allocations being determined by the weighting factor.

In the example in figure 5, it was determined that option A would satisfy objective 1 very well, so I allocated the maximum number of points available (50). However, option A hardly satisfies objective 2 but does satisfy it somewhat, so I have allocated it 5 points out of a maximum of 20. You should continue down the option A column until points are allocated to all objectives, then total the points for option A at the bottom of the column.

At this point, before you can really continue, you must know how to define each option in terms of substitution, utility versus direct value, and objective quantification. Then you will have a relatively unbiased method of decision making that will help you in setting priorities for your objectives and asset allocation processes.

Asset Allocation Options

Simply stated, an asset allocation option is a decision regarding how current assets and discretionary cash will be distributed to meet your objectives. The objective might be to purchase a new car: option A may be to purchase a Chevy, while option B may be to purchase a Mercedes. Although you might like to purchase the Mercedes, it would mean a need to allocate greater resources to this objective and less to other objectives. Since the Mercedes purchase would take too large an allocation of resources and could only be purchased if the other objectives are forsaken, you may decide against this option. However, you may also decide against the Chevy and purchase a Lincoln, thus creating option C.

Multiple solutions exist within an achievable, realistic range. Once these choices are reduced, they can be substituted and compared on the basis of utility (intangible) versus direct (tangible) value, to help you choose the best asset allocation option to meet your objectives. If you were trying to make a choice within only one objective, for instance, if you simply wanted to buy a car, you would not have to go through this process.

Pulling It All Together

In figure 6, you created a decision chart based on ten objectives. That chart determined the maximum weighting that was to be given each objective. In figure 7, already-completed decisions are indicated in the first three columns.

To complete the process, items that satisfy the corresponding objective are listed under each option in columns A, B, and C, and so on. At this point, we are concerned only with the options for each objective; we are not worried about whether it falls under option A, B, or C. In addition, only those items that are truly worth considering to satisfy each objective should be listed—not every item one can possibly think of. For instance, if you are considering a Lincoln, Mercedes, or Chevy, a Buick or Oldsmobile should not be listed if these are not viable alternatives.

Next, options for achieving each objective must be considered and points allocated to each item according to how well that item satisfies your desires (needs come into play after quantifying each item). Keep in mind the maximum points allowed for each item. In figure 7, the Mercedes scores a 50, the Lincoln gets a 40, and the Chevy gets only a 15. Obviously there is considerable subjectivity here. But you can easily see which items best satisfy your desires relative to each objective by looking

FIGURE 7 Asset Allocation Options Using Decision Matrix

Objective	Weight	Options A	B	C
1. New car	50	(50) Mercedes $40,000	(40) Lincoln $25,000	(15) Chevy $15,000
2. Boat	20	(20) 16 ft. $15,000	(10) 20 ft. $30,000	(15) 18 ft. $22,000
3. Comfortable retirement	80	(50) $4,000/mo. income $500,000	(70) $4,500/mo. income $550,000	(80) $5,000/mo. income $600,000
4. Funds for child's education	70	(65) U of I $35,000	(60) St. John's $25,000	(70) Harvard $50,000
5. Vacation home	30	(30) Florida condo $90,000	(20) Wisconsin cabin $60,000	(15) Bahamas condo $50,000
6. Sufficient money for spouse at death	90	(90) Pay all debts and have income $300,000	(50) Pay all debts $100,000	(70) Income $200,000
7. Braces for children	60	(60) Dr. X $2,000	(50) Dr. Y $1,500	(15) Dr. Z $1,000
8. Hair transplant for husband	0	(0) Dr. G	(0) Dr. H	(0) Dr. I
9. Entertainment center	40	(30) Sears $2,500	(40) Radio Shack $3,000	(25) K-Mart $1,500
10. Dog	10	(10) Setter $100	(5) Greyhound $60	(8) Beagle $75

at a chart and noting which item has the highest point allocation relative to each objective.

There is a cost, however, to achieve this utopia that has to be determined. Now go through your chart and note the dollars necessary to obtain each item.

Next, go back and make a similar asset allocation chart, except that this time the option A column will contain the items for each objective that were allocated the most points; this has been done in figure 8. Add up the costs of all option A's. Is the total within your financial limits? At

FIGURE 8. Sample Tally of Options

		Options		
Objective	Weight	A	B	C
1. New car	50	Mercedes $40,000		
2. Boat	20	16 ft. $15,000		
3. Comfortable retirement	80	$5,000/mo. income $60,000		
4. Funds for child's education	70	Harvard $50,000		
5. Vacation home	30	Florida condo $90,000		
6. Leave spouse sufficient money at death	90	Pay all debts and have income $300,000		
7. Braces for children	60	Dr. X $2,000		
8. Hair transplant for husband	0	N/A		
9. Entertainment center	40	Radio Shack $3,000		
10. Pet dog	10	Setter $100		
Total		$1,100,100.00		

this point, you need to know your financial limits, which are governed by current assets, current and anticipated discretionary cash flow, and anticipated income from outside sources, such as pension plans and trusts.

Your first choices will probably exceed your financial limits. You can now approach your decision in two ways. You may wish to proceed down column A and allocate resources to the items corresponding to the objectives with the highest priority (indicated by their weight) until all your resources are allocated; you would then disregard the achievement of the other objectives. Or, if you are like most people, you will want to make substitutions and create a new column B so you can meet other objectives. Your new column B will list a different combination of items, within your financial constraints, to meet your objectives. In addition, you may find it necessary to create new columns—C, D, and so on—to satisfy your objectives to different degrees.

Once completed, this chart will present several combinations of items that can satisfy your needs based on your finances. After all are considered, it will be possible to decide which is the preferred combination.

Once you have your objectives clearly in mind, you are well on your way to developing a working financial retirement plan.

THE THEORY BEHIND THE CONCEPTS

Substitution is the act of replacing one item with another. We normally substitute because we perceive a better value, lower cost, or some alternative benefit by using the substituted item. In our auto example, we substituted the Chevy for the Mercedes because of cost. We then substituted the Lincoln for the Chevy because of perceived value while still meeting our first substitution criterion of cost.

We must sometimes choose between alternatives whose values are intangible (utility value), as opposed to those whose values are tangible (direct). The value of allocating resources toward payment of insurance premiums is the intangible benefit of peace of mind brought about by the fact that the insured is protected against risk. Many times we must decide on whether to allocate our resources to an alternative with utility value (for example, insurance or a will) or direct value (for example, new kitchen cabinets or subscriptions to a few new magazines).

QUANTIFYING YOUR RETIREMENT LIFESTYLE

More than any single factor, money determines when people retire and the type of lifestyle they will have during retirement. The following method is designed to help you determine your income needs during retirement and create a plan to achieve your objective.

An Overview of the Process

The basic steps in the analysis can be summarized as follows:

1. Determine what your income needs would be if you were to retire today.
2. Determine the future value of those dollars upon retirement.

3. Calculate the amount of capital you will need at retirement to pro-
    duce the future income need over the course of retirement.
4. Subtract sources of income during retirement, expressed in terms of
    retirement-date dollars, from this capital need.
5. Subtract from this capital need all cash expected up to retirement
    age, any future contributions to retirement plans, and the future
    value of any current capital. (If you have a surplus, that's great!)
6. If more capital is required upon retirement, determine how much
    more must be saved each year to reach the required level.

Much of this analysis depends on certain formulas; these are summarized in figure 9. The variables in the formulas are described in the text,
since they will vary depending upon how they are used.

Finally, the analysis depends on many assumptions and parameters,
including the following:

- inflation rate
- after-tax rate of return
- age at death
- Social Security benefit amount and rate of increase
- income from employee benefit plans
- existing working capital (that is, assets that will increase in value and
  will be available at retirement to provide income)
- growth rate for existing working capital
- projected liabilities at age of retirement
- future annual contributions to employee benefit and retirement plans
- rates of return on future annual cash flow margin and future annual
  employee benefit and retirement plans

Determine these assumptions and parameters for your own situation;
growth and inflation rates should be realistic.

Your Income Needs

The first step in estimating your future income needs is determining your
present needs. To do this, you must create a budget or, rather, a summary
of what your current expenses are. Begin making a list of all expenses you
incur according to your current standard of living and record these along
the left-hand side of a piece of paper. Try to include as much detail as
possible and account for every expense, including income taxes. Add an
expense item labeled "Cash" to account for cash expenditures that you
cannot specifically retrieve from past records. The total from this column
should accurately represent your total current expenditures, which indi-
rectly represent the lifestyle you lead.

FIGURE 9. Planning for Retirement—An Overview

Step	Determination	Formula used
1	Current annual need: Determine income needs based on amount desired if you were to retire today	—
2	Future need: Determine future value of current annual need	Future value formula
3	Capital need: Determine what amount of capital upon retirement will produce future need over course of retirement	Present value of annuity due formula
4	Income sources: Determine sources in current dollars .... Determine future value of those sources ..... Determine value in retirement-age dollars of those sources over the time period in which they will be paid	— Future value formula Present value of annuity due formula
5	Subtract income sources from capital need	—
6	Determine future value of existing capital, cash flows until retirement, and value of future contributions to retirement plans	Future value formula
7	Subtract this from capital need: Surplus: You are on your way to financial independence .... Capital requirement: Determine how much must be saved to reach required level	— Future value of annuity due formula

The Formulas

Future value: $(1 + i)^n$

Present value: $\dfrac{1}{(1 + i)^n}$

Future value of annuity: $\dfrac{(1 + i)^N - 1}{i}$

Inflation adjusted rate (iar): $\dfrac{r - i}{1 + i}$

FIGURE 9.   Planning for Retirement—An Overview (concluded)

$$\text{Present value of annuity due: } 1 + \frac{1 - \dfrac{1}{(1 + iar)^{n-1}}}{iar}$$

i = inflation rate for income needs or expected annual return rate for income sources

n = number of years

r = postretirement expected rate of return

Notes on Assumptions

The following are some important considerations regarding the fundamental assumptions inherent in determining financial independence:

Annual basis compounding. All compounding of inflation and estimated annual increases is done on an annual basis. Even the monthly income needed and the monthly retirement benefits are converted to annual figures before their increases are applied. This simplifies the verification of numbers by hand, is easier to follow, and provides for easier implementation of the implied recommendations.
Income need or received occurs at the beginning of the year. A basic assumption is that any income need is "paid out" and any income source is "received" at the beginning of the year (an annuity due rather than an end-of-year assumption called a deferred annuity). This convention provides a conservative approach to the calculation of income need (there is no accumulation of interest on the unused portion during the year) but necessitates a more liberal approach to income received (you receive interest on the annual amount for the whole year). This allows the system to net the two flows directly and I feel it is sufficiently accurate when working with projected figures. However, you may wish to adjust your income need and income received downward slightly to compensate for this convention.
Conservation of capital in nominal dollars. Conservation of capital is in nominal as opposed to real dollars. In other words, the amount you specify to be conserved until mortality is to be stated in future dollars. The system does not adjust for the effects of inflation on that sum. This is something to keep in mind when entering the amount to be conserved.
It is possible to outlive capital required. A corollary to the previous statement, since capital is conserved in nominal dollars if you or your spouse live past the mortality age you use, it is possible for the capital provision for retirement to be completely exhausted. It is suggested that you be conservative both in your choice of a mortality age and in your determination of the capital to be conserved to mortality figure. Sufficient buffer is necessary should you be fortunate enough to outlive your "expected" mortality.

Now comes the creative part. Next to each expenditure listed, make an estimate of what you would like that expense to be if you were retired now, in today's dollars. For example, you might now spend $1,000 per year on vacations. However, if you were retired today, you might want to travel more, and thus allocate $3,000 per year (in today's dollars) to this expense during retirement. You may spend $2,500 per year on clothing now because of your employment, yet during retirement you estimate a need for less formal attire and allocate only $1,000 per year to this expense. The key here is to picture yourself retired, at this very moment, and create the expenditures you would like to have. Of course, you should be realistic with your wants.

This method allows you to create the lifestyle you would like during retirement by estimating now what your desired cash allocations will be at retirement. Too often, people retire, gather up all their assets, determine their monthly estimated income from Social Security and employee benefit plans and then create their lifestyle around what they have. They are then in a situation in which their finances control them and their lifestyles during retirement. Using the above method, you can quantify the lifestyle you would like during retirement and plan to accumulate the amount you will need to achieve that lifestyle.

Converting to Future Dollars

At this point you have an approximate gross (before tax) income need during retirement in today's dollars. We will call this the current annual need. Inflation, however, will erode this figure by the time you reach retirement age. Therefore, project this need out to your anticipated retirement date and beyond to determine its equivalent purchasing power in future dollars.

For example, John and Mary would like to retire when John is 60; he is now 53. They have determined that their gross annual income need for retirement in today's dollars is $30,000. Other assumptions and parameters are listed in figure 10.

The future need to maintain today's buying power will be the result of applying the future value formula to the current annual need. In this instance, the n in the formula represents the number of years from today until retirement; the i represents the assumed rate of inflation, in this instance 6 percent. Figure 11 presents the future need assuming a 6 percent inflation rate for various points in John and Mary's retirement years. It indicates that they will need $45,109 when John reaches 60 to equal the buying power in today's dollars.

FIGURE 10. John and Mary's Planning Parameters

General:

Annual income required* (before tax)	$30,000	
Inflation rate	6%	
Capital funding approach	Deplete	

	Preretirement	Postretirement
Annual rate of return (before tax)	10.00%	10.00%
Marginal income tax rate	42.00%	n/a**
Annual rate of return (after tax)	5.80%	n/a

Personal:		John	Mary
Retirement age		60	57
Expected mortality age		89	88
Social Security*:		$9,936	$4,968
Age range		65–89	65–88
Annual Increase		2%	2%
Earned income*:		$100,000	—
Age range		53–59	—
Annual increase		6%	—
Retirement income*:			
Defined benefit		$6,000	—
Age range		65–89	—
Annual increase		0%	—

---

*Stated in current dollars.
**Here, we are assuming a constant marginal rate.

Determining Capital Needs

Once the future need has been determined, John and Mary need to determine how much they will need upon retirement to sustain the future need each year for all the years of retirement. This can be determined by applying the formula for the present value of annuity due; the *n* in this formula is the number of years for the period, which in this case is from retirement age until death.

If you look at this formula in figure 12, you will note that instead of *i* for an inflation rate, *iar* is used. This is the inflation adjusted rate and is the real rate of return expected over the period in question, which in this

FIGURE 11. **Future Income Needed to Maintain $30,000 Income in Current Dollars (Based on 6% annual inflation)**

Years from today	Year	John's age	Future annual income needed
0	1986	53	$30,000
1	1987	54	31,800
2	1988	55	33,708
3	1989	56	35,730
4	1990	57	37,874
5	1991	58	40,147
6	1992	59	42,556
7	1993	60	45,109
8	1994	61	47,815
9	1995	62	50,684
10	1996	63	53,725
11	1997	64	56,949
12	1998	65	60,366
13	1999	66	63,988
14	2000	67	67,827
15	2001	68	71,897
16	2002	69	76,211
17	2003	70	80,783
18	2004	71	85,630
19	2005	72	90,768
20	2006	73	96,214
21	2007	74	101,987
22	2008	75	108,106
23	2009	76	114,592
24	2010	77	121,468
25	2011	78	128,756
26	2012	79	136,481
27	2013	80	144,670
28	2014	81	153,351
29	2015	82	162,552
30	2016	83	172,305
31	2017	84	182,643
32	2018	85	193,602
33	2019	86	205,218
34	2020	87	217,531
35	2021	88	230,583
36	2022	89	244,418
37	2023	—	259,083
38	2024	—	274,628

FIGURE 12.   Determining John's and Mary's Capital Needs—The Phases

Phase 1:	John will be 60 through 64; Mary will be 57 through 61			*Assumed iar* in pva due formula*
Current annual income need		$ 30,000		
Inflated at 6% for 7 years		45,109		
Capital required to produce this inflated need			$ 209,727	3.77%
Phase 1 net capital required at John's age 60			$ 209,727	

Phase 2:	John will be 65 through 67; Mary will be 62 through 64			*Assumed iar* in pva due formula*
Current annual income need		$ 30,000		
Inflated at 6% for 12 years		60,366		
Capital required to produce this inflated need			$ 174,592	3.77%
Less:				
Social Security—				
John		$ 9,936		
Inflated at 2% for 12 years		12,601		
Capital value of this inflating income			$ 35,121	7.84%
Less:				
Defined benefit plan		$ 6,000		
Inflated at 0% for 12 years		6,000		
Capital value of this noninflating income			$ 16,413	10.00%
Phase 2 net capital required at John's age 60 (but in age-65 dollars)			$ 123,058	
Discounted at 10% for 5 years to John's age 60			$ 76,409	

Phase 3:	John will be 68 through 89; Mary will be 65 through 86			*Assumed iar* in pva due formula*
Current annual income need		$ 30,000		
Inflated at 6% for 15 years		71,897		
Capital required to produce this inflated need			$1,101,911	3.77%
Less:				
Social Security—				
John		$ 9,936		
Inflated at 2% for 15 years		13,373		
Capital value of this inflating income			$ 148,952	7.84%

FIGURE 12.   Determining John's and Mary's Capital Needs—The Phases (concluded)

Phase 3: (continued)

Less:			
Social Security—			
Mary	$ 4,968		
Inflated at 2% for 15 years	6,686		
Capital value of this inflating income		$ 74,476	7.84%
Less:			
Defined benefit plan	$ 6,000		
Inflated at 0% for 15 years	6,000		
Capital value of this noninflating income		$ 57,892	10.00%
Phase 3 net capital required at John's age 60			
(but in age-68 dollars)		$ 820,591	
Discounted at 10% for 8 years to John's age			
60		$ 382,812	

Phase 4:	Mary will be 87 through 88		*Assumed iar* in pva due formula*
Current annual income need	$ 30,000		
Inflated at 6% for 37 years	259,083		
Capital required to produce this inflated need		$ 508,744	3.77%
Less:			
Social Security—			
Mary	$ 4,968		
Inflated at 2% for 37 years	10,337		
Capital value of this inflating income		$ 19,922	7.84%
Phase 4 net capital required at John's age 60			
(but in Mary's age 87 dollars)		$ 488,822	
Discounted at 10% for 30 years to John's age			
60		$ 28,014	

Capital required		
Phase 1	$ 209,727	
Phase 2	76,409	
Phase 3	382,812	
Phase 4	28,014	
Total capital required at John's age 60	$ 696,962	

---

*iar: Inflation-adjusted rate. The assumed inflation rate or real rate of return for the period, determined according to formula in Figure 9.

instance starts at the retirement date. The reason for using this is straight-forward. The future-need figure has already been adjusted for any infla-tion between now and retirement age; the inflation adjusted rate accounts for inflation after retirement. For the *iar* formula, *r* is the before-tax, postretirement expected rate of return, and *i* is the annual inflation rate.

We now have a figure that accurately reflects capital needs at the be-ginning of retirement. From this, we must subtract all income sources over the course of retirement.

Determining Value of Sources of Income

The value of income sources is determined in the same manner in which we determined need. First, these sources are totaled in current dollars. The future value of those dollars is determined using the future value for-mula, where *n* is the number of years between now and retirement, and *i* is the estimated annual increase (or return) for the source.

The value of this income source at the beginning of the retirement period is determined by applying the present value of annuity due for-mula. Here, again, *iar* adjusts the figure for inflation that occurs after the retirement date; for the *iar* formula, *i* is the estimated annual increase (or return rate) for the income source. In the present value of annuity due for-mula, *n* represents the number of years over which the income is received.

The difference between the income need and all the income sources is the total capital required at retirement.

Retirement Phases

Figure 12 presents an example of the calculations involved in determining capital needs. The example recognizes the fact that many factors, such as income requirements, Social Security benefits, and income from retire-ment plans, will change during retirement. Therefore, the retirement years in the example have been divided into four phases: phase 1 lasts five years; phase 2 lasts three years; phase 3 lasts 22 years; and phase 4 lasts two years, ending with Mary's estimated date of death at age 89.

For each of the phases, both income needs and sources have been de-termined as described earlier. In phase 2, John is 65 through 67 years old. The future value (upon retirement) of his currently desired $30,000 in-come is $60,366. The next calculation is the amount of capital required upon retirement age to produce this amount of income for the next three years of this phase, when he turns 68; this turns out to be $174,592. The income source over this three-year time period is worth $9,936; the future value of this source when he turns 65 will be $12,601. The total value of this source of income for this three-year phase, using the present value of annuity due formula, is $35,121. Similarly, his pension plan will be worth $16,413. The income sources, when subtracted from income needs, produce a net capital requirement of $123,058.

The capital needs for the different phases reflect values at the start of that phase. For instance, $123,058 represents the capital needed by John when he is 65. However, the overall planning process is based on John's retirement age of 60. Therefore, when the final tally is made, the capital needs of the individual phases must be restated in age-60 dollars. The present value formula accomplishes this. For phase 2, that discounted amount is $76,409.

If income sources over a particular phase produce a surplus over income needed, that surplus is carried over to the next phase as an income source. However, its value at the beginning of the next phase must be determined by using the future value formula: n is the number of years between the two phases, or the age at the beginning of the next phase less the age at the beginning of the current phase; i is the expected rate of return for that period.

The bottom of figure 12 presents a summary of the capital amounts necessary in each phase. The final sum is the total capital required at retirement, when John is 60.

Taking Stock of Existing Capital

Up to this point, we have taken future income needs, subtracted all future income sources available during retirement, and arrived at a lump sum of capital required at retirement.

But what about existing capital and future sources of income that will accumulate before retirement?

Figure 13 continues the John and Mary example, with these new figures included. John's and Mary's current capital is determined, and its value upon retirement is calculated using the future value formula; r is the assumed rate of return on the capital. From this figure, all liabilities remaining at retirement are subtracted. This produces a future value for existing working capital. In the same way, future values are determined for any future annual cash flow and future contributions to any qualified retirement plans. In determining future values for cash flow, you should remember to use an after-tax rate of return. These future values are then totaled.

FIGURE 13.   Determining Capital Needs—The Final Calculations

Capital required at John's age 60		$696,962
Sources of Capital		
Existing working capital:		
Today's value	$350,000	
Potential value at age 60 (7% annual growth)	$562,024	
Less: Liabilities at age 60	$ 0	
Subtract existing capital		562,024
		$134,938
Future annual cash flow:		
Today's value	$ 24,000	
Potential value at age 60* (5.8% after-tax return)	$200,227	
Future contributions to qualified retirement plans:		
Annual contribution	$ 8,000	
Potential value at age 60** (10% before-tax return)	$ 82,154	
Subtract cash flow, retirement contributions		$282,381
Total capital surplus		**$147,443**

*Assuming an annual increase of 0% in the amount John will invest.
**Assuming an annual increase of 3% in the amount contributed.

Capital Required upon Retirement

The future value of net existing capital and the future values of annual cash flows and pension contributions are subtracted from the lump sum of capital required upon retirement. This is the figure you have been working toward: the total capital required or surplus.

If there is a total capital requirement, you will need to determine a schedule of savings for this amount.

Annual investing schedules are calculated by dividing the total capital required by the factor determined in the future value of annuity formula, where i is the after-tax rate of return [(1 – marginal tax bracket) × rate of return], and n is the number of years before retirement age (retirement age less current age).

Once calculated, the annual investment schedules will tell you how much additional savings will be necessary each year to achieve your objective.

If you showed a capital surplus on your financial independence calculation, as did John and Mary, you are on your way to achieving your objective.

PLANNING YOUR RETIREMENT INCOME

Although many of us believe there is a possibility we may never retire, statistically the likelihood is that we will retire at some point in time. At the close of the last century, 68 percent of males 65 years or older were still working. In 1954, this had decreased to 39 percent. By 1963, the figure had dropped further to 24 percent, and today only five percent to 10 percent of men over 65 still go to work each weekday morning. This trend shows that fewer and fewer individuals actually plan on having careers that continue past the age of 65. Therefore, it is imperative to determine your sources of income during retirement.

What Are the Sources of Your Income?

A study by The Social Security Administration to track the income of those over 65 showed these sources: 34 percent came from Social Security; 29 percent from earned income, with people still working full- or part-time; 15 percent from accumulated capital; 7 percent from public pensions; 5 percent from public assistance; 1 percent from contributions from others; and 2 percent from all other sources. Note that, of all the sources, only two can realistically be controlled. In others words, if you are working, it is possible to take measures to increase your earnings, and there are steps you can take to increase your accumulated capital and make it more productive. The other sources listed are really not under your control. This study verifies the importance of planning for your income during retirement.

Since only 15 percent of the income of the average retired person comes from the capital he or she has accumulated, it is extremely important to keep total income in line with current living costs. You must be able and willing to change many habits or ways of thinking that may stand in your path of becoming financially independent.

Calculating Your Future Income

Before you can begin to make the necessary adjustments and/or changes to your current asset situation, you need to have an idea of what income you need, not only now but in the future. A simplified analysis is provided in figure 14 to help you get a future picture of what your income flow may look like and how long it may last.

In the example, I am assuming that retirement is about to begin immediately. For this reason, I began with a current asset listing of lump sums of dollars available to provide income. These lump sums are from a number of different sources. There is a thrift plan, a profit-sharing plan, a PAYSOP (which is a stock accumulation plan), a NOW savings account, and two individual retirement accounts (IRA). The total value of these assets in the example is $88,184.

The next step was to project income needs and future sources of income. From these figures, I determined the annual surplus or deficit. The surpluses were added and the deficits subtracted from the balance of the asset account, which was gradually depleted to determine how long into the future the income would last.

In the example, the couple determined that they needed $57,217 in today's dollars to continue in a lifestyle to which they are accustomed (the income need in 1987 is $57,217). I assumed a 5 percent inflation rate on this income need, so the amount increases by that percentage each year. This number can change up or down depending on what projection you feel comfortable with. I then subtracted Social Security benefits and also the fixed pension amount that would be coming in; Social Security benefits were projected to increase at a 2 percent rate. Historically, a 3 percent increase would probably be more accurate, but I chose to take the conservative rate. The total of Social Security and pension payments represents the annual income. In 1987, the amount of income available is $62,652. The income need was then subtracted from the annual income; in the first year, this led to a surplus of $5,435. The surplus was then added to the previous asset balance. The asset balance was also assumed to grow at an annual growth rate of 7 percent, so by the end of 1987, the couple has a total asset balance of $100,172. For simplicity, the surplus was added to the balance, and the total was compounded at the assumed 7 percent growth rate. This, however, implies that the surplus or deficit exists for the entire year. In fact, it would accumulate over the course of the year. A more conservative course would be to assume half the growth rate (3.5 percent) for the surplus or deficit; an even more conservative course would be to add the surplus or deficit after the growth in the balance has been determined.

FIGURE 14.   Retirement Analysis of Current Assets and Future Needs and Income Sources

Current Assets

Available assets	*Value (as of 1/1/89)*
Thrift plan	$23,264
Profit-sharing plan	38,608
PAYSOP	2,386
NOW account	12,000
IRA/Sam	7,423
IRA/Norma	4,503
Total	**$88,184**

Future needs and income sources

Year	Income need	Pension	Social Security	Total annual income	Annual surplus (deficit)*	Balance**
1989(3)	63,082	50,592	12,547	63,139	57	117,972
1990(4)	66,236	50,592	12,798	63,390	(2,846)	123,185
1991(5)	69,548	50,592	13,054	63,646	(5,901)	125,494
1992(6)	73,025	50,592	13,315	63,907	(9,118)	124,522
1993(7)	76,676	50,592	13,582	64,174	(12,503)	119,861
1994(8)	80,510	50,592	13,853	64,445	(16,065)	111,062
1995(9)	84,536	50,592	14,130	64,722	(19,813)	97,636
1996(10)	88,762	50,592	14,413	65,005	(23,758)	79,050
1997(11)	93,200	50,592	14,701	65,293	(27,907)	54,722
1998(12)	97,860	50,592	14,995	65,587	(32,273)	24,020
1999(13)	102,754	50,592	15,295	65,887	(36,867)	(13,746)
2000(14)	107,891	50,592	15,601	66,193	(41,698)	(59,325)
2001(15)	113,286	50,592	15,913	66,505	(48,781)	(113,533)
2002(16)	118,950	50,592	16,231	66,823	(52,127)	(177,256)
2003(17)	124,898	50,592	16,556	67,148	(57,750)	(251,456)
2004(18)	131,142	50,592	16,887	67,479	(63,664)	(337,178)
2005(19)	137,700	50,592	17,225	67,817	(69,883)	(435,555)
2006(20)	144,585	50,592	17,569	68,161	(76,423)	(547,817)
2007(21)	151,814	50,592	17,921	68,513	(83,301)	(675,297)
2008(22)	159,404	50,592	18,279	68,871	(90,533)	(819,439)
2009(23)	167,375	50,592	18,645	69,237	(98,138)	(981,807)
2010(24)	175,743	50,592	19,017	69,609	(106,134)	(1,164,097)
2011(25)	184,531	50,592	19,398	69,990	(114,541)	(1,368,142)

Growth assumptions
Income needs: 5%
Social Security: 2%
Balance: 7%

*Annual surplus/(deficit) is added to asset balance.
**Balances are as of end of year.

The analysis was continued in the example into the year 2011, or 22 years into the future. As you can see, by the year 1990, the couple will begin to show a deficit when netting out the income need against the annual income available. In that year, the couple will start to draw on their asset balance if they want to continue at their current lifestyle.

You can also see in this example that by the year 1999, the couple will start seeing a deficit in their total asset balance, meaning of course that they have spent all of their available capital. If they are uncomfortable with this result, they will have to make adjustments.

As you can see, this analysis is useful when determining at what age you might wish to retire. It may also help you determine whether you want or need to adjust your income needs downward by possibly cutting expenses, or it may show that you need to earn a slightly higher rate of return than what you thought you would need to safely project into the future.

Most of us would want at least part of our money to outlast us and to provide a cushion for late-in-life contingencies; under no conditions would we want to be dependent upon others. Achieving the balance that is right requires some good planning and possibly a little luck. Spending in addition to saving is perhaps the real financial challenge for our later years, and financial planning is essential both before and after retirement.

NOTES: RETIREMENT PLANNING CLARIFICATIONS

Social Security for Mary after John's death

For simplicity's sake, we assumed that Mary's Social Security spousal benefit of one-half would hold throughout retirement. In reality, it would change to the full widow's benefit after John's death, in Phase 4.

Income Taxes in the Post-Retirement Period

There is an allowance for income taxes in the postretirement period. The future annual income need of $30,000 is gross income required, before tax, in today's dollars. The figure is arrived at by estimating expenses, including income taxes. Thus, as the future annual income need is inflated, the allowance for the income taxes is inflated also.

Formulas

If you are using a financial calculator to calculate the present value of annuity due, *n* is correct for number of years in the period. However, make sure that your calculation is assuming that the payments are made at the beginning of each year.

Existing Working Capital and Future Annual Cash Flow Margin

These numbers as well as liabilities at retirement are determined on a case-by-case basis. In the example, existing working capital only included investable assets that we determined would grow at a 7 percent after-tax rate (based on the type of assets involved). Future annual cash flow margin was arrived at by setting up a regular investment program to be earmarked for retirement.

Clarifying the Calculations

To clarify the calculations we used in determining John's and Mary's capital needs, we have provided the calculations used to determine the capital required to meet income needs during phase 2. Remember, we are trying to determine what amount of capital at John's current age of 53 will produce enough income to meet John's and Mary's inflated income needs when John is 65 through 67 (a three-year time period). We have already determined that, in today's dollars, John and Mary would need $30,000 each year to meet their needs. We have also assumed a 6 percent rate (*i*) and a postretirement expected rate of return (*r*) of 10 percent.

Phase 2:

Current annual income need: $30,000
Inflated at 6 percent for 12 years (N=12 years): $60,366
    To arrive at the inflated future income need, use the future value (FV) formula:

$$FV = PV (1 + i)^N = 30,000 (1 + 0.06) = 60,366$$

where

        PV = present value of the current annual income need
        n = number of years
        i = interest rate

Capital required to produce this inflated need: $174,592

To arrive at this figure, you must first determine the inflation adjusted rate (*iar*):

$$iar = \frac{r-1}{1+i} = \frac{0.10 - 0.06}{1 + 0.06} = 0.0377 = 3.77\%$$

You then must use the Present Value of Annuity Due (PVAD) formula to determine the capital requirements:

$$PVAD = 1 + \frac{1 - \dfrac{1}{(1+iar)^{N-1}}}{iar} \times FV$$

$$PVAD = 1 + \frac{1 - \dfrac{1}{(1+0.377)^{3-1}}}{0.0377} \times 60{,}366$$

$$PVAD = 2.892328857 \times 60{,}366 = 174.598^*$$

*Differences may be due to rounding.

In this example, we have carried out the calculation to nine decimal places. You may get slightly different answers if you round off any part of the calculation. Because we are solving for the 3-year time period from and including age 65 to age 67, in this equation N=3 years.

PART

Preparing Your Financial Strategies for Today and Tomorrow

4

Taking Financial Inventory

Most people are careful about maintaining bits of information and records concerning their personal data and financial status. However, most people are not very conscientious when it comes to keeping their financial information organized. Too often, the material is scattered in files or drawers, recorded in places that may be forgotten, or jotted down on scraps of paper that have yellowed with age. When the person or the person's family is suddenly confronted with the need for basic information that is necessary to resolve physical and financial problems that inevitably occur, the material is often difficult to locate.

In addition to the commitment to keep information up to date, one needs a system for organizing and tracking it.

If you take the time to fill in all the blanks of the following Inventory of Personal and Financial Data (figure 15), you will have everything in one place, and you will be in a better position to review and evaluate your own position. Also, if ever you are temporarily incapacitated or unable to handle matters because of illness, your family will be able to keep things flowing smoothly.

The time that you spend on the inventory now will certainly be worth the effort later. Remember also to check the information from time to time to be certain the inventory is current. This record should be transcribed to worksheets and kept with your important papers.

WHY KEEP RECORDS?

Many people never keep organized financial records because they never consider the consequences of *not* doing so. Financial record-keeping, tracking, and review offer a sense of direction. Assuming you have set quantifiable goals, record-keeping allows you to track your progress toward achieving those goals. Your records become a personal library of your financial accomplishments and a motivating tool for further achievement. In addition, these records become your family's survival kit in case of your death. Upon your death, one of the most difficult tasks for uninformed family members who are currently in a state of emotional shock is to organize and assimilate often confusing financial information. By keeping proper records, you will do much to minimize the pain and confusion often associated with this task. Keep these records at home, with a second copy in your safe-deposit box.

HOW TO BEGIN

As you first sit down to tackle this task, realize that you need to plan for updating and reviewing. Schedule time in your calendar for this, preferably every six months. This is not to say that this should be the only time to change your records. Ideally, all records should be brought up to date as events occur that warrant such changes. However, all financial records should be reviewed at least every six months and adjusted accordingly.

To begin your record-keeping, start with the Personal Financial Statement. This includes a listing of your total assets, total liabilities, and net worth (assets minus liabilities). This form will be valuable in tracking your financial progress. The financial statement gives you a "snapshot" of your financial situation at a particular time. A series of these statements will be akin to the frames of a motion picture. Each frame shows a particular scene, but the frames, when run together, tell a story; your series of financial statements will tell your financial story.

In addition, you will find it handy to have a current financial statement on hand for those times when your banker or accountant needs it. It is much easier to make adjustments and keep your statement current than it is to have to create a statement from scratch each time it is needed.

Continue your record-keeping by filling in the blanks for the following forms included in figure 15:

- savings and checking accounts
- certificates of deposit
- stock investments and/or mutual fund shares
- corporate and government bond holdings, U.S. Treasury bills and notes
- U.S. savings bonds
- real estate holdings (including your [home])
- collectibles and valuable possessions
- inventory of the contents of your home
- individual retirement account
- retirement plans
- personal and family information
- document locator
- safe-deposit box
- your professional consultants
- local offices: Social Security and Internal Revenue Service
- wills
- trusts
- life insurance policies
- annuities inventory
- health insurance
- residential insurance
- automobile insurance
- credit cards
- capital improvements in your home
- register of securities purchased and sold
- capital gains or losses
- quarterly income report

FIGURE 15. Inventory of Personal and Financial Data

Personal Financial Statement

NAME _____

ADDRESS _____

CITY _____

STATE _____ ZIP _____

PHONE NUMBER _____

MONTH _____ DAY _____ 19 ____

ASSETS	AMOUNT	LIABILITIES	AMOUNT
Cash on hand and in banks		Notes payable to banks	
U.S. government securities—see schedule		Secured	
Listed securities—see schedule		Unsecured	
Unlisted securities—see schedule		Notes payable to relatives	
Accounts and notes receivable		Notes payable to others	
Due from relatives and friends		Accounts and bills due	
Accounts and notes receivable		Accrued taxes and interest	
Due from others—good		Other unpaid taxes	
Accounts and notes receivable		Mortgages payable on real estate—see schedule	
Doubtful			
Real estate owned—see schedule		Chattel mortgages and other liens payable	
Real estate mortgages owned			
Automobiles		Other debts—itemize	
Personal property			

FIGURE 15. Inventory of Personal and Financial Data (continued)

Other assets—itemize				
			TOTAL LIABILITIES	
			NET WORTH	
TOTAL ASSETS			TOTAL LIABILITY AND NET WORTH	

SOURCES OF INCOME	
Salary	$
Bonuses and commissions	$
Dividends	$
Real estate income	$
Other income—itemize	
TOTAL	$

CONTINGENT LIABILITIES	
As endorser or comaker	$
On leases or contracts	$
Legal claims	$
Provision for federal income taxes	$
Other special debt	$

PERSONAL INFORMATION	
Business or occupation	Age
Partner or officer in any other venture	
Married	Children
Single	Dependents

GENERAL INFORMATION
Are any assets pledged?
Are you defendant in any suits or legal actions?
Personal bank accounts carried at
Have you ever taken bankruptcy?
Explain:

FIGURE 15. Inventory of Personal and Financial Data (continued)

SCHEDULE OF U.S. GOVERNMENT SECURITIES, STOCKS, AND BONDS OWNED

Description	In name of	Market value

SCHEDULE OF MORTGAGES OWNED

Description of property covered	Date of acquisition	In name of	Maturity	Amount

SCHEDULE OF REAL ESTATE OWNED

Description of property and improvements	Date of acquisition	Title in name of	Cost	Market value	Mortgage Amount	Maturity

FIGURE 15.   Inventory of Personal and Financial Data (continued)

SCHEDULE OF LIFE INSURANCE CARRIED

Amount	Name of Company	Beneficiary	Cash surrender value	Loans

BANKS OR FINANCE COMPANIES WHERE CREDIT HAS BEEN OBTAINED

Name	High Credit	Basis

Date signed _____ 19 _____

_____
Signature

FIGURE 15. Inventory of Personal and Financial Data (continued)

SAVINGS AND CHECKING ACCOUNTS

Savings and Checking Acounts	Name of bank	Address of bank	Account number	Individual or joint account* (name[s])	Location of passbook or checkbook	Balance as of (date)
Savings Account						
Savings Account						
Savings Account						
Checking Account						
Checking Account						
Money Market Account						
Money Market Account						
NOW Account						
NOW Account						

*Many banks freeze a joint account when one of the joint owners dies. If this is your bank's policy, it is suggested that each spouse set up a separate account in his or her name in addition to a joint account.

FIGURE 15. Inventory of Personal and Financial Data (continued)

CERTIFICATES OF DEPOSIT (CDs)

Amount and maturity date	Name of bank or institution	Address of bank or institution	Account number

STOCK INVESTMENTS AND/OR MUTUAL FUND SHARES

Name of company or fund	Number of shares owned	Serial number	Date acquired	Cost per share	Total cost	Owner(s)

FIGURE 15. Inventory of Personal and Financial Data (continued)

CORPORATE AND GOVERNMENT BOND HOLDINGS, U.S. TREASURY BILLS AND NOTES

Issuer	Type	Interest rate	Number owned	Serial number	Purchase price	Date bought	Maturity date	Owner(s)

U.S. SAVINGS BONDS

Type (Series E, H, EE, HH)	Serial number	Denomination	Owner(s)	Location

FIGURE 15.   Inventory of Personal and Financial Data (continued)

	REAL ESTATE HOLDINGS (including your home[s])		
	Property 1	Property 2	Property 3
Description of property and address			
Form of ownership (solely or jointly owned)			
Date acquired			
Original cost			
Down payment			
Current market value			
Original amount of mortgage			
Term of mortgage			
Monthly payment			
Maturity date of mortgage			
Name of mortgagee (lender)			
Name(s) of owner(s)			

FIGURE 15.   Inventory of Personal and Financial Data (continued)

COLLECTIBLES AND VALUABLE POSSESSIONS

Item	Description of item	Original value	Current value	Date acquired	How acquired: purchase, gift, or inheritance	Location
1						
2						
3						
4						
5						
6						
7						
8						
9						
10						
11						
12						

FIGURE 15. **Inventory of Personal and Financial Data** (continued)

INDIVIDUAL RETIREMENT ACCOUNT (IRA)

Name	Name of bank or institution	Address of bank or institution	Account number	Location of passbook, certificate, or receipt	Balance as of _____ (date)

FIGURE 15. Inventory of Personal and Financial Data (continued)

INVENTORY OF THE CONTENTS OF YOUR HOME

An updated inventory of the contents of your home should be maintained for insurance purposes as well as for estate planning. Using the format suggested below for the living room, prepare a worksheet for a detailed listing. A similar listing should be prepared for the dining room, master bedroom, second bedroom, third bedroom, bathrooms, den or library, kitchen, basement, attic, and garage. It is also recommended that photographs showing the contents of each area be available. You should also prepare a list for each of the following: jewelry, clothing, silverware, dishes, stemware, table and bed linens, personal belongings, and any other valuable possessions, such as art, antiques, and cameras.

Area	Contents	Date Acquired	Cost	Current Value

FIGURE 15.   Inventory of Personal and Financial Data (continued)

RETIREMENT PLANS		
	Name	**Name**
Are you are member of a retirement plan? (yes, no)		
If yes, name of company or plan		
Address		
Telephone number		
Pension number		
Currently receiving pension benefits from the following company or plan		
Address		
Telephone number		
Pension number		
Other information, notes		

FIGURE 15. Inventory of Personal and Financial Data (continued)

PERSONAL AND FAMILY INFORMATION		
		Date
	Name	**Name**
Full legal name		
Address: number and street		
city, state, zip code		
Birth date		
Place of birth		
Father's name		
Mother's name		
Social Security number		
Current marriage: Date of marriage		
Place of marriage		
Date of termination (death or divorce)		
Divorce: Name of previous spouse		
Date of divorce		
State of jurisdiction		
Marital status (single, married, widowed, separated)		
Military service: Branch		
Serial number		
Date of entry		
Date discharged		
Place discharged		
Disability (service connected)		

FIGURE 15. **Inventory of Personal and Financial Data** (continued)

CHILDREN, INCLUDING THOSE LEGALLY ADOPTED				
Full name	Full address	Birth date	Place of birth	Extent of dependence

EMPLOYERS (LAST 10 YEARS)		
	Name	Address
Current or last employer (Dates: from _____ to _____)		
Previous employer (Dates: from _____ to _____)		
Previous employer (Dates: from _____ to _____)		
Previous employer (Dates: from _____ to _____)		

FIGURE 15.   Inventory of Personal and Financial Data (continued)

DOCUMENT LOCATION		
	Name	Name
Item(s)	Location of document	
Birth certificate		
Marriage certificate(s)		
Divorce papers		
Adoption papers		
Naturalization papers		
Social Security card		
Passport		
Military records		
Will: Original		
First copy		
Second copy		
Paid bills		
Past tax returns		
Cancelled checks		
Stock and bond certificates		
Certificates of deposit		
Insurance policies: Life		
Automobile		
Homeowner's		
Health		
Pension documents		
Bank books		
Real property documents		
Deed to cemetery plot		

FIGURE 15. **Inventory of Personal and Financial Data** (continued)

SAFE-DEPOSIT BOX		
Every household should rent at least one safe-deposit box for storing important documents and valuable jewelry. Items to be kept in your safe-deposit box include certificates of birth, marriage, divorce, and death; military discharge papers; stock and bond certificates; pension, Keogh and IRA information; certificates of deposit; naturalization papers; copyrights and patents; adoption papers; deeds; mortgages; and jewelry. Your will should be kept in a box rented in your spouse's name, and your spouse's will should be kept in a box rented in your name. Usually, a bank seals a box as soon as it learns that the owner has died. It is important to note that the contents of a safe-deposit box are not insured. If you wish to insure the contents of your box, you can purchase a separate policy or a rider to one of your other policies. Enter below the information pertaining to your safe-deposit box.		
Information About Safe-Deposit Box(es)	Box 1	Box 2
Name of bank where it is located		
Address of bank		
Box number		
Name of deputy who has access to box		
Address of deputy		
Location of key		
Inventory of contents		

FIGURE 15. Inventory of Personal and Financial Data (continued)

YOUR PROFESSIONAL CONSULTANTS			
Consultant	Name	Address	Phone
Accountant			
Lawyer			
Broker			
Banker or trust officer			
Insurance agent _____ (type of coverage)			
Insurance agent _____ (type of coverage)			
Doctor (internist)			
Doctor _____ (specialty)			
Doctor _____ (specialty)			
Dentist (general)			
Clergyperson			

FIGURE 15.   Inventory of Personal and Financial Data (continued)

LOCAL OFFICES: SOCIAL SECURITY AND INTERNAL REVENUE SERVICE
Social Security Office
Enter here the address and phone number of your local Social Security office. If you are in doubt, check your phone book under *Social Security Administration.*
Number and Street
City   State   Zip Code
Phone Number
It is suggested that you phone the Social Security office before you go there. You may be helped on the phone. Even if you must appear in person, your individual circumstances may require specfic information that you would then be prepared to provide.
Internal Revenue Service Office
Enter here the address and phone number of your local Internal Revenue Service office. If you are in doubt, check your phone book under *U.S. Government, Internal Revenue Service.*
Number and Street
City   State   Zip Code
Phone Number

FIGURE 15.   Inventory of Personal and Financial Data (continued)

	WILLS	
	(Name of husband or individual)	(Name of wife or individual)
Have you made a will? (yes, no)		
If yes, date of will		
Executor: Name		
Address		
Telephone number		
Alternate Executor: Name		
Address		
Telephone number		
Have you prepared a supplemental letter of instructions? (yes, no)		
If yes, note location of the supplemental letter*: Original		
First copy		
Second copy		

*Should be attached to original, first copy, and second copy of your will.

FIGURE 15.   Inventory of Personal and Financial Data (continued)

	(Name of husband or individual)	(Name of wife or individual)
TRUSTS		
Have you created a trust? (yes, no)		
If yes, type (living, testamentary)		
Date created		
Name of attorney		
Address of attorney		
Telephone number of attorney		
I am beneficiary of the following trust:		
Name of trustee		
Address of trustee		
Telephone number of trustee		
Notes		

FIGURE 15.   Inventory of Personal and Financial Data (continued)

	LIFE INSURANCE POLICIES		
	Policy		
	1	2	3
Name of insured			
Name of company			
Policy number			
Type: term, cash value, endowment, specialized			
Face amount			
Beneficiary(ies)			
Current loan, if any			
Current cash value, if any			
Premium amount			
Premium due date(s)			
Name of insurance agent			
Address of agent			
Telephone number of agent			
Location of policy			

FIGURE 15.   Inventory of Personal and Financial Data (continued)

ANNUITIES INVENTORY			
	Annuity		
	1	**2**	**3**
Name of annuity owner			
Name of company			
Address of company			
Premium amount			
Premium due date(s)			
Payout plan			
Income per month			
Beneficiary(ies)			
Survivor's rights (yes, no)			
Name of agent			
Address of agent			
Telephone number of agent			
Location of policy			

FIGURE 15.   Inventory of Personal and Financial Data (continued)

HEALTH INSURANCE	
Medicare Claim number	
Hospital insurance (Part A):	_____ _____ Effective date Effective date
Medical insurance (Part B):	_____ _____ Effective date Effective date
Medigap insurance Name(s) of insured	
Name of company	
Address of company	
Policy number	
Coverage dates: from–to	
Risks covered, and deductible amount of each	_____ $_____ _____ _____ $_____ _____ _____ $_____ _____ _____ $_____ _____ _____ $_____ _____
Premium amount	$
Premium due date(s)	
Name of insurance agent	
Address of agent	
Telephone number of agent	

FIGURE 15. Inventory of Personal and Financial Data (continued)

Other health coverage	Company	Policy number	Premium amount	Premium due date
Basic hospitalization			$	
Basic medical/surgical			$	
Supplementary hospitalization			$	
Comprehensive major medical			$	
Catastrophic major medical			$	
Long-term care			$	
Disability income insurance			$	
Dental insurance			$	
Optical expense benefits			$	
Hearing aids			$	
Prescription drug plan			$	
Blood program			$	
Additional information, notes				

FIGURE 15.   Inventory of Personal and Financial Data (continued)

RESIDENTIAL INSURANCE	
Name of company	
Address of company	
Policy number	
Coverage dates: from–to	
Risks covered, and deductible amount of each	_____ $_____ _____ _____ $_____ _____ _____ $_____ _____ _____ $_____ _____ _____ $_____ _____
Premium amount	$
Premium due date(s)	
Name of insurance agent	
Address of agent	
Telephone number of agent	
Additional information, notes	

FIGURE 15.   Inventory of Personal and Financial Data (continued)

AUTOMOBILE INSURANCE	
Car or cars insured	
Name of company	
Address of company	
Policy number	
Coverage dates: from–to	
Risks covered, and deductible amount of each	_____ $ _____ _____ _____ $ _____ _____ _____ $ _____ _____ _____ $ _____ _____ _____ $ _____ _____
Premium amount	$
Premium due date(s)	
Name of insurance agent	
Address of agent	
Telephone number of agent	
Additional information, notes	

FIGURE 15.   Inventory of Personal and Financial Data (continued)

CREDIT CARDS			
Issuer's name	Account number	Issuer's address	Issuer's phone

FIGURE 15.   Inventory of Personal and Financial Data (continued)

CAPITAL IMPROVEMENTS IN YOUR HOME		
Date	Capital Improvement	Cost

Keeping a permanent record of the capital improvements you have made in your home will help minimize the amount of capital gains subject to tax when you sell your home.

FIGURE 15. Inventory of Personal and Financial Data (continued)

SECURITIES PURCHASED AND SOLD REGISTER

This form covers ☐ common stocks ☐ preferred stocks ☐ debentures ☐ bonds

PURCHASES

Date	No. of Units	Certificate Number	Unit Price	Tax	Broker's Commission	Cost	Total Investment	Dividend Rate	Dividend Yield

FIGURE 15.   Inventory of Personal and Financial Data (continued)

Date	No. of Units	Certificate Number	Unit Price	Tax	Broker's Commission	Amount Received	Profit Or Loss

SALES

FIGURE 15. Inventory of Personal and Financial Data (continued)

CAPITAL GAINS OR LOSSES

For the Period from _____ to _____

#	Issuer Of Security	Number Of Shares	Date Purchased	Date Sold	Total Cost Of Purchase	Total Amount Of Sale	Held Less Than 12 Months		Held More Than 12 Months	
							Short-Term Capital Gain	Short-Term Capital Loss	Long-Term Capital Gain	Long-Term Capital Loss
1										
2										
3										
4										
5										
6										
7										
8										
9										
10										
11										
12										
13										
14										
15										
16										
17										
18										
19										
20										
S										
T										

Notes:

FIGURE 15.   Inventory of Personal and Financial Data (concluded)

QUARTERLY INCOME REPORT

This page covers the following: ☐ common stocks   ☐ preferred stocks   ☐ debentures   ☐ bonds

Name Of Issuer	No. Of Shares	1st Quarter		2nd Quarter		3rd Quarter		4th Quarter		Total
		Date/Rate	Amount	Date/Rate	Amount	Date/Rate	Amount	Date/Rate	Amount	

5

Insurance and Risk Management

Risk is an everyday life factor for every person, business, or organization. Generally, risk has to do with the uncertainty of loosing, or not gaining, something of value. Risk occurs because of variations in outcomes or results. Without risk there would be no need for insurance. Insurance is a system for reducing risk.

There are two basic kinds of economic risk: speculative risk and pure risk. Speculative risk involves the chance of loss or gain, whereas in pure risk, there is only the chance of loss or no loss.

Pure risks are "pure" in the sense that they do not mix both profits and losses. Insurance is concerned with the economic problems created by pure risk. There are several different types of insurance to manage various insurable risks.

LIFE INSURANCE

If life is long and healthy, and if the rate of investing and rate of return on investment exceeds or equals projected needs, you should be in good shape by retirement. However, if death occurs before or even during retirement and prior to the time you have been able to accumulate sufficient assets, a severe financial setback could occur.

Life insurance was created to prevent this situation. In this respect, life insurance is really the purchase of time. A premature death takes away the time an individual would have to accumulate assets for future use. Life insurance creates those dollars that would have been created and establishes a fund for the dependent survivors' financial needs. It has the same effect during retirement by allowing the survivors the opportunity to cover any outstanding debts or obligations with insurance proceeds instead of having to reduce the assets that are currently being used to provide income.

Since you don't know how long you will live, you should definitely have a plan in the event death occurs before you have had time to accumulate a living estate.

With life insurance, as with all types of insurance coverage, you must spend money only to buy protection against the loss of something of measurable value. Life insurance should be the economic extension of yourself. You must insure to protect something that you either have or are aiming to acquire. You should not be planning to protect something that you would like to have that is otherwise unobtainable. This is absolutely fundamental to proper risk management. Paying for excess coverage of any type automatically saps the current cash flow that could otherwise be used to build assets more quickly and less expensively—assets that are needed to provide for the present or to create a secure financial basis for your retirement. Remember, it is always possible that you will not become disabled or will not die earlier than life expectancy tables predict.

You have to prepare for that and leave enough discretionary dollars to accumulate for those future needs. However, it would be a mistake to direct all cash flow to extra living expenses and investments and none to insurance policies, for this assumes that you will never sustain a loss of property, lose good health, become disabled, or die before an average life expectancy. The two extremes are always invalid assumptions for everyone.

Calculating Your Life Insurance Needs

How do you calculate the amount of life insurance that you should carry? First of all, not everyone needs life insurance. It may not be necessary for those without dependents, or those with businesses that would not suffer in their absence. The ultimate objective in financial planning is reached at a point when no life insurance is needed at all. However, in the meantime, life insurance should be viewed as protection for accumulation and/or estate liquidity. Protection for asset accumulation and estate liquidity are the two major needs that life insurance is normally meant to meet. It is necessary to measure the difference between what one has now and what one needs now in case of death. This is called capital-needs analysis. Harold Gourges, author of *The Financial Planning Handbook*,[1] has devised a simple method to do this. Using his method, we can address insurance needs as related to many specific objectives, such as college education, mortgage, and dependents income under one comprehensive system. You can assess your financial needs at your death, determine what assets are available to provide for those needs, and then use life insurance to provide the difference.

To demonstrate the process, we will use Harold's example of a 35 year-old couple, Cheryl and Mel Coleman, and their two children, Gary, 11, and Kathy, 13. Inflation will be intentionally ignored for the moment.

Step One: Capital Needs for Family Income.   Most families will maintain their standard of living with about 75 percent of the budget used prior to the death of a breadwinner. That, then, can be used as a rough guideline for this step (see figure 16). An exact amount can be arrived at by using figure 17. That worksheet is ideally suited for measuring and then updating income needs in the event of death.

The Colemans have determined that, if Mel dies now, Cheryl and the two children will require 75 percent of their current living expenses of $32,000, or $24,000 per year. From this income requirement, you must subtract Social Security income benefits, which will vary in each case. For the family as a whole, as of the first half of 1982, the maximum Social Security benefit for the surviving parent and two or more children is $1,079 per month. The surviving parent and one child would receive $925. One surviving child would receive $460. This is tax-free income, and it must be subtracted from the after-tax income needs.

The Colemans would initially receive the maximum amount of Social Security income, $12,950 per year, but this amount would decrease as the children leave home for college. In discussing this problem, Cheryl decided that, if it were not for the extra expenses for the children, she would not actually need the Social Security income. The Colemans must therefore subtract the initial $12,950 benefit from the annual after-tax need of $24,000. They must also subtract any private pension income, computed on an estimated after-tax basis, that the dependents would receive. They

[1]New York Institute of Finance, 1983.

FIGURE 16   Capital Needs Worksheet

1. Capital needs family income:		
After-tax income needs	$ 24,000	
Less: estimated Social Security benefits	(12,950)	
Pension income	0	
Income needs from investment capital	11,050	
Capital needed assuming 8% after tax return	$138,125	
2. Capital needs for debt repayment:		
Home mortgage	$ 0	
Charge cards	500	
Bank notes	7,000	
Other	0	
Total debts	$ 7,500	
3. Other side funds:		
Emergency reserves	$ 48,000	
College education funds	50,000	
Other	0	
Total	$ 98,000	
4. Estate settlement costs:		
Funeral expenses	$ 5,000	
Administration and probate	4,500	
Federal estate taxes	0	
State death taxes	0	
Uninsured medical costs	1,000	
Other		
Total	$ 10,500	
5. Total capital needs		$254,125
6. Current assets available or convertible to income-producing investments	$ 20,300	
7. Lump-sum distributions from qualified retirement plans:		
IRA	0	
Keogh	0	
Pension	0	
Profit-sharing	$ 12,000	
Other	0	
8. Current life insurance	$125,000	
9. Total capital available		$157,300
10. Net capital needs (surplus): capital needs less capital available		$ 96,825

FIGURE 17 Monthly Expense Worksheet

EXPENSES	JAN	FEB	MAR	APR	MAY	JUN	JUL	AUG	SEP	OCT	NOV	DEC	TOTAL
1 Moving expense													
2 Employee business expense													
3 IRA													
4 IRA—spouse													
5 KEOGH													
6 KEOGH—spouse													
7 Interest penalties													
8 Alimony payments													
9 Federal income tax													
10 State income tax													
11 Local income tax													
12 Other withholdings													
13 Social security													
14 Property tax													
15 Charitable contributions													
16 Union dues													
17 Financial services													
18 Bank charges													
TOTAL EXPENSES—THIS PAGE													

Monthly Expense Worksheet (continued)

EXPENSES	JAN	FEB	MAR	APR	MAY	JUN	JUL	AUG	SEP	OCT	NOV	DEC	TOTAL
19 Rent													
20 Mortgage principal													
21 Mortgage interest													
22 Second home principal													
23 Second home interest													
24 Other interest													
25 Homeowner's insurance													
26 Auto insurance													
27 Health insurance													
28 Life insurance													
29 Disability insurance													
30 Liability insurance													
31 Other insurance													
32 Home repair													
33 Auto repair													
34 Auto expense													
35 Licenses													
36 Auto loans													
TOTAL EXPENSES—THIS PAGE													

Monthly Expense Worksheet (continued)

	EXPENSES	JAN	FEB	MAR	APR	MAY	JUN	JUL	AUG	SEP	OCT	NOV	DEC	TOTAL
37	Other loans													
38	Other loans													
39	Charge cards													
40	Savings													
41	Investments													
42	Child support													
43	Care for other dependents													
44	Domestic help													
45	Doctors													
46	Dentists													
47	Medical—prescriptions													
48	Medical—other													
49	Electricity													
50	Gas													
51	Water/sewer													
52	Trash removal													
53	Miscellaneous utilities													
	TOTAL EXPENSES—THIS PAGE													

Monthly Expense Worksheet (concluded)

EXPENSES	JAN	FEB	MAR	APR	MAY	JUN	JUL	AUG	SEP	OCT	NOV	DEC	TOTAL
37 Telephone													
38 Gifts													
39 Food—at home													
40 Food—out													
41 Clothing													
42 Cleaning/laundry													
43 Personal care													
44 Pet care													
45 Entertainment													
46 Vacations													
47 Hobbies/recreation													
48 Books/magazines/newspapers													
49 Education													
50 Allowances													
51 Allowances													
52 Appliances													
53													
54													
TOTAL EXPENSES—THIS PAGE													
TOTAL EXPENSES													

will also sometimes have a choice of receiving a lump-sum or installment payment from such a qualified pension plan. That decision will depend on their relative income and estate tax brackets. In most instances, except where the estate tax bracket is relatively high, they will want to take a lump-sum distribution and show its estimated amount in step seven.

The Colemans do not expect a regular pension income from their employer but do anticipate a lump-sum distribution from a profit-sharing plan.

The Colemans' income need from investment capital is, therefore, $11,050 ($24,000–$12,950). Assuming an after-tax return of 8 percent, $138,125 of capital is needed to maintain adequate family income.

Step Two: Capital Needs for Debt Payments. The next step is to deal with debts outstanding at the time of death. Refer to figure 16 to see the Colemans' Capital Needs Worksheet.

Typical debts include the home mortgage, charge cards, auto loans, and bank notes. Mel Coleman has factored this monthly payment into his survivors' income needs and, therefore, makes no provision for it in this step. This same recommendation generally applies. It is not wise to pay off long-term debt on a home, which is a reliable inflation hedge, in today's inflationary environment. However it would be wise to pay off major short-term liabilities, such as credit card debt, bank demand notes, or auto loans.

The Colemans have decided that an auto note of $7,000 and $500 credit card debt—a total of $7,500—should be paid off if he should die.

Step Three: Other Side Funds. Two particular lump-sum needs appear in most financial plans. There is the ever-present need for emergency cash reserves. The income produced by these reserves must be automatically reinvested to hedge against inflation damage to their emergency buying power. This is why these reserves are set up as a separate category and are not included in the capital needed for family income. Most families will need emergency reserves of between 50 percent and 100 perent of their annual after-tax income needs.

The Colemans are very conservative and indicate a need for $48,000 of emergency cash reserves.

In addition, Cheryl and Mel have estimated that their children will each need $25,000 in today's dollars for college education at the state university. Assuming that a side fund for that purpose could be invested to grow with rising costs, they decide on an educational fund of $50,000, or a total of $98,000 for other side funds.

Step Four: Estate Settlement Costs. The average funeral expense of middle- to upper-middle-class Americans is estimated to be $5,000. The Colemans agree. Administration and probate is approximately 4½ percent of gross taxable estate, which should not include the proceeds of life insurance. The Colemans' gross taxable estate is $100,000, and they, therefore, allot $4,500 for this expense.

Mel Coleman has no federal estate liability (of course, if Cheryl died first, this would be altered).

Because state death taxes vary so greatly, it is assumed here that Mel Coleman is not liable. You should check your situation with regard to state taxes, since state laws vary.

It is impossible to predict uninsured medical expenses. If a person dies of an illness, the estate will be billed for any medical costs not covered by hospital and medical policies. Health coverage should be checked very carefully. Even with a comprehensive plan, $5,000 should be set aside for uninsured medical expenses. The Coleman's health coverage is adequate, and $1,000 is set aside for this eventuality.

Estate settlement costs, therefore, total $10,500.

Step Five: Total Capital Needs. Total capital needs are determined by adding the bottom-line figures derived in steps one through four. The Colemans have estimated needs for family income of $138,125, needs for debt payment of $7,500, side-fund needs of $98,000 and estate settlement costs of $10,500—for capital needs of $254,125.

Step Six: Current Assets Available for Income Production. Step six must total all investment assets currently available for income production or convertible to income-producing investments. At this time, the Colemans find their current assets consist of $3,500 cash in a savings account, plus $16,800 they have accumulated in growth mutual fund shares. This total of $20,300 is all the assets that could easily be used to create income or to provide side funds.

Step Seven: Lump-Sum Distributions from Qualified Retirement Plans. Next, lump-sum distributions expected from all qualified retirement plans must be totaled. Because decisions as to how and when such assets will be distributed are not usually made in advance, the total is shown here, as opposed to appearing as regular income in step one.

Mel Coleman has built up $12,000 of capital in his current employer's profit-sharing plan over the past 11 years. He expects his estate to accept it as a lump sum void of any income or estate taxation, since he has named his wife as beneficiary.

Step Eight: Current Life Insurance.   Now you must add the proceeds the immediate family, or the insurance trust, is expected to receive for life insurance policies. The proceeds of any policies owned by the spouse, children, or trusts, or that were given to others three years before death, are not included in the estate. These proceeds should, however, be available for the dependents' capital needs.

Mel Coleman's group insurance policy totals twice his annual $50,000 salary, or $100,000. It was assigned to his wife and is, therefore, not included in his estate. Even had it been, after his transfer credit and/or the marital deduction it would not have produced any estate taxes. In addition, he owns a $25,000 whole life policy with $6,080 cash value. His family's life insurance proceeds, therefore, total $125,000.

Step Nine: Total Capital Available.   The total capital available is determined by adding the bottom line figures in steps six, seven, and eight. The Colemans have $20,300 of "living" assets available for producing income: $12,000 from a profit-sharing plan, and $125,000 of current life insurance. This total of $157,300 would be available to offset their capital needs.

Step Ten: Net Capital Needs (Surplus).   You now determine the crucial number that tells whether one is underinsured or overinsured. Subtract the total from step nine (capital available) from the total from step five (capital needs), and you have the answer. The Colemans have capital needs of $254,125 (step five) and capital available of $157,300 (step nine), for a net capital need of exactly $96,825. They should round upward to the nearest $5,000 and, therefore, immediately purchase $100,000 of annual renewable term insurance.

The capital needs worksheet (figure 16) is completed for the Colemans as a summary of our ten-step method of diagnosing Mel's life insurance needs.

It must again be emphasized that the two chief causes of a capital gap are (1) insufficient investment assets and (2) severe erosion of the assets already accumulated by estate settlement costs.

In the case of the Colemans, the gap of $96,825 is clearly the result of a lack of current assets available or convertible into income-producing investments. Time and a financial plan should allow the Colemans' to increase these assets and thereby reduce the family's need for life insurance.

For others, the major cause of a capital gap is often the erosion of assets caused by estate-settlement costs. With passing time, uncertain investment success, and inflation, the problem could get worse. This would be especially true if capital needs for family income, debt repayment, and other side funds grew as rapidly as did the available capital.

It is best to ignore inflation and use only the current picture for the purpose of computing the capital gap or surplus. In other words, future insurance needs should be determined by computing a new capital needs analysis at least once a year. That alone will reliably determine the proper level of life insurance.

As the estate grows, the capital-needs analysis often points toward increasing estate settlement costs. To avoid these costs, one may decide to pay an insurance company in advance, by increasing life insurance coverage, to allow the estate to pass without shrinkage.

Major Classes of Life Insurance

There are two major classes of life insurance: individual and group. Individual insurance involves a separate policy contract for each purchaser. Group life insurance usually involves one group contract for many individuals, usually taken out by employers.

Individual Life Insurance.   Individual life insurance is issued on the basis of individual applications through life insurance agents and may be adapted to almost every insurance need. Today it accounts for about 50 percent of all life insurance in force. It is usually written in units of $1,000. Premiums are computed on an annual basis but may be paid monthly, quarterly, semiannually, or annually. Premiums are due and collectible at the home office or the branch office of the insurer.

Group Life Insurance.   Group life insurance is the most recent and most rapidly growing major class of life insurance. It differs from ordinary life insurance in that the unit covered is the group rather than the individual. Most group plans are sold to employers for their employees, but others are also sold to creditors, unions, trusts, and associations. Almost all the insurance is term insurance, purchased for a stated time period.

Basic Types of Life Insurance Contracts

A great many different life insurance policies are offered to meet the varying needs of individuals. All are either whole life, term, or endowment policies or a combination of one or more of these. Three contracts are basic to life insurance: whole life insurance, term insurance, and endowment insurance.

Whole life insurance includes those forms in which the face amount is paid on the death of the insured whenever death occurs. This is a permanent form of insurance and covers the insured for life. Term insurance pays on the death of the insured only if the insured dies during the term covered. If the insured outlives the period, there is no obligation on the part of the insurer with respect to benefits of any kind. Endowments provide insurance coverage during a stated period and emphasize the savings element. The face of the policy is payable at the end of the endowment period to the insured if living, or to the beneficiary if the insured dies during the period.

These three basic contracts form the foundation of the many life insurance coverages offered in the market. No matter how complex a coverage may seem or how many benefits or options are available, the policy achieves its objectives by incorporating in a single contract the features of one or more of the basic contracts.

In forms of insurance other than life, the contingency insured against may or may not happen. The policies are issued for a term and may run to expiration with no claim made. Some life policies are written for a term; many are not. Many life insurance contracts are written on a permanent or whole life basis; if such contracts are kept in force, the benefits provided must ultimately be paid. Life insurance policies thus are classified as permanent and temporary. Temporary, or term, life insurance provides protection only for the number of years designated in the contract. It is more like the usual insurance contract covering property. Permanent, or whole, life insurance forms the basis of many insurance programs, while term insurance provides temporary protection.

Whole Life Insurance Policies.   Whole life insurance may be written on a straight life basis, on a limited-payment basis, or on a single-premium basis. The whole life contract known as the straight life policy is also known as the ordinary life policy. It provides for the periodic payment of premiums as long as the insured lives. Benefits are payable at the death of the insured, though a policyholder may stop paying premiums and take the accumulated equity in the form of cash or a reduced paid-up policy.

A whole life form known as the limited-payment policy provides for premium payments for a designated term or until the prior death of the insured. At the end of the premium-payment term, the insurance is paid up for the life of the insured. Under the single-premium policy, the premium is paid at the outset of the policy term in a lump sum, but most contracts are paid for with periodic installments. When no more premiums are payable on a contract, it is called a paid-up policy.

On the assumption that the payment of a single premium is a limited-payment policy with payments limited to a period of a year, it may be stated that whole life forms may be reduced to two classes: straight life and limited-payment life. When two or more lives are covered in one policy, the term *joint life* is applied to the contract.

In all of these forms, the policy matures only on the death of the person whose life is the subject of the insurance; termination of the policy prior to death through cancellation or surrender of value precludes, of course, a death settlement.

During the past decade, the use of the various types of contracts has changed. As a total, the ordinary insurance types have slightly more than doubled, while total group insurance in force increased more than three times in the same period. Within the ordinary class, the limited-payment life, paid-up life, and endowment contracts are decreasing in popularity, while the popularity of term life insurance has increased substantially, along with universal life contracts, in which premium amounts and death benefits can be changed periodically.

The ordinary life policy is used not only for protection but also as a means of savings. The policy values are available to the policyholder when the need for insurance protection has been outlived. Even on contracts calling for continuous premium payments to death, the insured may stop payments at any time. On retirement, the policyholder may elect to discontinue premium payments on permanent insurance and take cash or keep a substantial amount of insurance in force; or if preferred, the cash value may be used to augment retirement income by electing an annuity settlement instead of cash.

The flexibility of the whole life contract accounts for its appeal: The contract is permanent unless the premium is not paid. Although the net protection element decreases (face value less cash value) as the older ages are reached, the insured have long-term protection for such purposes as last expenses, income to beneficiaries, or estate liquidity. Future uninsurability, the attainment of advanced age, or other contingencies cannot terminate the protection. There is no necessity for conversion or for redrawing the plan to keep the insurance for life.

The ordinary life policy is issued on a level-payment premium basis, and the premiums continue throughout the lifetime of the insured. Many object to the requirement of the ordinary life policy that premiums be paid until death. In the declining years of a life, productive capacity diminishes, so it is sometimes considered desirable that premium changes cease after a certain age is reached.

Limited-Payment Policies. The limited-payment whole life contract provides for the payment of the face of the policy upon the death of the insured. It differs from the ordinary life policy in that premium payments are charged for a limited number of years only. After the stipulated number of annual premiums have been paid—the more usual number being 10, 20, or 30—the policy becomes a fully paid-up policy. Some are paid up at the specified age of a holder, such as 65 or later.

Frequently, policyholders confuse the limited-payment life policy with an endowment form, and after making the stipulated payments, they expect to receive the face of the policy from the insurer. The face of the policy is not paid until the death of the insured, though the cash and loan values are higher than under an ordinary life form; the difference depends upon the number of payments called for in the contract. Obviously, the fewer the payments, the faster the reserve will accumulate during the premium-payment period. Therefore, a greater reserve will be found under a limited-payment life policy than under an ordinary life form.

Under the limited-payment form, a policyholder who dies during the early policy years will have paid more than for an ordinary life policy. On the other hand, the policyholder may find sufficient compensation for the extra outlay in the knowledge that at a later age, when income will be curtailed, the burden of paying life insurance premiums will also be eliminated.

In arranging the life insurance program, the question of the relative merits of the ordinary life policy and the limited-payment life policy is inevitable. There is no arbitrary advantage of one over the other. As a general rule, when funds available for insurance premiums are scarce, the ordinary life form will prove preferable, since more insurance may be obtained for the amount available for premiums. Moreover, if the economic status of the insured improves, the insurance may be rearranged to a limited-payment plan.

If cost is not a determining factor in the life insurance program, the insured may wish to eliminate further life insurance premium payments upon retirement through the limited-payment life policy.

The single-premium policy is the extreme of the limited-payment contract. The premium under this contract is paid in a single sum. Because such premiums represent substantial amounts of money, most people are unwilling to take the risk of the large single payment. The policies do meet a need, however, in that they provide persons with an opportunity to provide for some future purpose in a manner that requires no further annual premium payments. Gifts or charitable bequests of life insurance are examples.

Modified Life Policies.   Offsetting the advantages of the ordinary life policy (moderate cost, level premium, and the savings element) are certain shortcomings. There is a tendency for those influenced primarily by cost and for those with large protection needs, such as young families, to be attracted from the ordinary life policy to the term policy. To supply an immediate permanent policy with an initial premium that is lower than the ordinary life premium, a modified life policy is offered by many companies. For a three- or five-year period the cost is lower than that of the ordinary life policy; thereafter, it is slightly higher.

Term Insurance Policies.   The earliest form of life insurance on record provided insurance only for a stated period, or term. Today term insurance is one of the most popular contracts. Term insurance is precisely what the name implies—insurance for a term, or temporary period. This may be contrasted to whole life insurance, which is permanent insurance and covers the insured as long as he or she lives. If term insurance is written for a year, it provides protection equal to the face of the policy for one year, no longer. If it is written for five years, the insurance covers for five years. At the end of the term—whether for one year, five years, or any period—coverage terminates, and the policy has no value whatever: If death occurs, the policy pays in accordance with its terms. If the insured does not die, the premium paid is fully earned by the underwriter, and at the end of the term the insurer is under no obligation to the insured.

When protection for a limited period is the element sought in the purchase of a policy, term insurance meets the requirement of the lowest possible immediate cash outlay. The low premium charge on term insurance reflects the limited time covered by the policy. In particular, it reflects the fact that the higher percentage of deaths occurring in the higher age brackets are not covered by the temporary protection of term insurance.

In light of the low cash outlay required for immediate protection, particularly in the younger age groups, term insurance is recommended to provide temporary insurance where the need for large amounts of protection is created by special situations. Sometimes only term insurance will provide sufficient amounts of life insurance to meet the consumer's large needs.

One of the principal uses of term insurance is to provide protection during a period of unusual financial strain. An individual may assume heavy obligations as part of a business venture. An untimely death and forced liquidation might seriously cripple the business. The prudent businessperson will frequently buy a term policy to cover the amount of the unusual liabilities for the length of time that is required for their liquidation.

Term insurance is also used to provide a fund for the liquidation of some particular debt. Frequently a term policy is carried in connection with a mortgage loan upon the home, with the insurance amount decreasing as the loan decreases. In order to see that dependents have a home without encumbrances in the event of the death of the wage earner, a term policy is carried to provide the necessary funds for liquidation. With the growing number of two-income families, new policies are now available so that both wage earners can be included in joint mortgage-redemption life insurance contracts.

Because of the apparently low premium in the earlier years, the attraction of term insurance is entirely forgotten in the later years of life. In the earlier years, the insured is in a better income position to pay the premiums, but the premiums are low because the probability of death during these years is slight. As the insured reaches the age when earnings have a downward trend, premium charges for term insurance rise very rapidly. Policyholders tend to discount the high premiums of later years as too remote to be of importance when, in their younger years, they are attracted to term insurance by the comparatively low premium charges. There is a tendency toward wholesale abandonment of the term insurance plan when premiums reach a level that the insured cannot or will not pay.

It is sometimes said that term insurance is an inferior type of coverage, and that a "cheap" coverage cannot be the better product that a higher premium will buy. The reasoning is not sound. The term contract is as safe, as adequate, and in every sense as satisfactory for the purposes for which it is devised as any contract offered by life insurance companies.

It is also wrong to say that everyone should automatically buy term policies and invest the difference. For policyholders, such a system rests on several fallacies. Term insurance cannot always be purchased, for poor health or older age makes it either difficult or impossible to buy. In addition, the difference between the cost of permanent and temporary protection cannot always bring greater returns at comparable safety, for this depends on size, diversification, costs, taxes, timing, types, and many other features of the alternative investment program.

No life insurance company or agent should have the slightest objection to a term policy in those situations where its use is indicated. It is not the term policy to which opposition is expressed but its misuse. Term insurance was not designed to be permanent insurance. For temporary protection to cover temporary needs, the policy is admirable. For careful use in connection with moderate-length investment programs, it may be beneficial. To augment a permanent life insurance plan during a period when the need for coverage is greatest, term insurance is indicated. A number of combination policies have been worked out by life insurers making judicious and generous use of term coverage.

Endowment Insurance Policies.   The ordinary life policy provides for the payment of the amount of the insurance to a designated beneficiary upon the death of the insured. The pure endowment reverses the process and pays the amount of the insurance only in the event that the insured lives a specified term. The amount of the insurance is paid to the insurer, if the insured is living at the end of the period; otherwise, the insurer pays nothing. There are few uses for pure endowments. Sometimes they are written for a child's education or for other specific purposes. Under the form, nothing is paid if the insured dies before the end of the period.

Most endowment policies offered by insurers incorporate the features of a term life insurance policy. When so written, if the insured dies during the term, the amount of the insurance is payable to a designated beneficiary. If living at the end of the period, the insured receives the amount.

Endowment insurance is written under a number of different forms, each designed to meet particular needs. The terms for which they are written may vary from five to 40 years, or they may be written to mature at a designated age, such as 60 or 65 years. There are also limited-payment endowments. For example, an endowment payable at death or at the end of 40 years may be written so that premium payments stop at the end of 20 years.

Variable Life Insurance.   Another innovation in life insurance is the variable life insurance contract. Early progress was blocked by legal complications, but in 1976 the Securities and Exchange Commission ruled that life insurance contracts with an equity base would be subject to the Securities Act of 1933–1934 and the Investment Company Acts of 1940. This ruling complicated the marketing of such contracts, for agents must also be licensed as security salespersons, and a prospectus with much detailed information must be given to the prospective buyer. This slowed the development of such contracts.

The fundamental idea is a modification of traditional (fixed-dollar-value) whole life insurance, in which the insurer pays a stated face value. In a whole life policy, this specified face value does not attempt to guarantee any particular purchasing power for the customer. In an era of continuing inflation, this is a real disadvantage to the life insurance beneficiary.

To offset this disadvantage, the variable life contract bases its reserves and policy amount-payable on investments that are devoted primarily to common stocks. The theory is that as inflation boosts common stock values and dividends in a separate account maintained for the variable life policies, the dollar values paid under the contract will also increase. It is hoped that increases will counterbalance decreases in the purchasing power of the dollar. The death payments are guaranteed not to fall below a minimum face value, but could increase if the equity values increased. Cash values are not guaranteed, however, and loan values are usually only 75 percent of the cash values instead of the full amount.

The stimulus for variable life insurance appears to have been based on two conditions: inflationary pressures that have eroded the real value of fixed-benefit contracts, and a shift in consumer preference away from secure investments to more speculative investments.

The potential disadvantages of variable life insurance should not be minimized. The fixed guarantees of traditional life insurance have provided security for consumers. Misunderstandings as to how much the variable life values might decrease (or might not be as large as expected) if equity returns are not favorable could endanger this. Expected policy loan values may not be available to policyholders. The increasing complexity of the contracts, with several different systems for systematically adjusting the face value, could increase confusion about life insurance.

The variable life product will probably include most of the features of fixed-benefit life insurance (except fixed cash values), and most observers predict that variable life insurance in time may comprise a significant portion of the life insurance sold in the United States.

Adjustable Life Insurance.   In the late 1970s, the adjustable life contract was introduced. This type of policy enables consumers to customize coverage based on their changing lifestyles. Like variable life policies, you can modify your coverage as your needs change. However, instead of having the life insurance amount vary with the prospective increased earnings of an equity-based account, the policyholder makes the choices on changing the policy amount upward or downward.

The usual whole life and term types of insurance are combined, with a wide flexibility as to when and how changes can be made. Most important, the premiums can be changed as well as the insured values. This is accomplished by increasing or decreasing the length of the term coverage, or by reducing or lengthening the premium-paying period of the whole life coverage.

In addition, the policy amounts can be increased by several methods. Two of them are traditional methods already used in many other life insurance contracts. The new feature is cost-of-living increases, by which the insured up to age 55 is permitted to buy additional life insurance every three years, without a medical examination. The increases are limited and are reduced by life insurance amounts purchased through other contracts.

The adjustable life contract can help solve the problems of the changing needs of consumers, the effect of inflation on fixed-dollar life insurance values, and the dispute over term versus whole life insurance. The adjustable life contract may have some of its own problems, but it may enable the consumer to save some of the time and costs of buying new policies or dropping old, separate policies.

The most difficult problem is probably the increased difficulty of understanding a more complicated product. However, adjustable life insurance avoids the dual-regulation (SEC and state insurance departments) problem of variable life insurance. Because of this, the application of the adjustable concept may be one of the most significant changes for life insurance in the 1980s.

Special Riders and Policy Combinations

A number of special riders are available in policies; consumers can also obtain numerous policy combinations to meet their specific needs.

Guaranteed Purchase Option.   Under the guaranteed purchase option, the policyholder is guaranteed the right, without medical examination, to increase the amount of his or her life insurance at standard rates at specified times or ages.

Some insurers permit six options to have four-year option intervals. Others permit the options to be exercised upon the marriage of the insured and at the birth of each child. One disadvantage of the purchase option is its relative inflexibility as compared with comparable term insurance amounts. The options can be exercised only at the stated ages or events, in the specified amount and in the form of a whole life contract.

The time eventually comes when many persons become partially or totally uninsurable because of physical deterioration or other changes. The applicant may obtain some insurance, as an impaired risk, for more than the standard rates, but total uninsurability prevents the further purchase of any life insurance. The guaranteed purchase option provides protection against the possibility of being forced to pay more than the standard rates, and guarantees the availability of insurance regardless of impairment.

Accidental Death and Dismemberment. This rider, or additional clause, allows for the payment of an additional benefit equal to the face amount of the policy if death occurs through accidental means. In addition, there is some benefit for dismemberment or loss of eyesight. If a person is properly insured, this additional rider is not needed, since the cause of death does not determine the amount of proper protection. Your dependents will not benefit from the extra money if you die in a plane crash rather than from a heart attack.

Life Insurance for Children. In most cases, the only additional financial obligation incurred upon the death of a child is for final expenses. The death of a child does not create loss of income and a need for dependency income unless, of course, your child is a source of support. A life insurance policy on the life of a child is rarely the best alternative investment consideration. Consider using the cash flow that would otherwise go toward a child's insurance premiums to fortify your own insurance program.

Some Final Thoughts on Life Insurance

Your life insurance program should be designed to fit your needs at this particular point in time. If your needs change from year to year, your policy should be reviewed accordingly. Please remember that insurance policies are not secret instruments never to be changed. Your need for protection may be less, the same, or more each year. Policies can be changed and riders can be dropped. A good insurance program should not be expensive. If properly designed, it should be well within your family's budget.

If, as you reach retirement age, your assets aren't sufficient to allow survivors to maintain their standard of living, settle your debts, pay for funeral and related expenses, and cover estate taxes, you should carry some form of life insurance.

DISABILITY INSURANCE

Disability, due to illness or accident, can be defined as temporary or permanent inability to work resulting in loss of earned income. For retirees who are living on other than earned income, there should be no need for this type of insurance. However, many retirees may still have some income coming in from outside employment. The question becomes, "If I became disabled now, how much of my earned income from work would I still need to continue to be able to live the lifestyle I choose to live?"

Calculating Your Disability Insurance Needs

We must first address the question of how much disability insurance is needed. For this, we will use a method similar to that used earlier to determine your retirement lifestyle. In the disability scenario, you will determine your disability lifestyle. Having completed the expense worksheets (figure 17), you should now go down each expense item and make an adjustment for that item with disability in mind. Ask yourself, "How much would I spend on this item if I were disabled?"

After completing this list, add the remaining numbers to come up with an amount that tells you what amount of total monthly or annual income you would need to continue in your chosen lifestyle if you were disabled. From this amount, subtract all income sources that are not related to income earned from work (investment income, Social Security, pension income, and so on). The net amount left will be the amount that cannot be covered by other income sources. This is the amount that you will need to cover with disability insurance. Be aware, however, that the insurance company may not be willing to write the amount of insurance that you feel you need. Most companies will only insure up to 65 percent of an individual's earned income.

If you are not yet retired, you can complete the above analysis in the same manner, making adjustments assuming that less of your income would come from sources other than earned income.

Let's work through an example. Allan and Betty Clark are currently retired and wish to determine the amount of disability insurance that Allan should continue to carry during retirement. Allan is currently working part time and earning $1,000 a month, but most of his retirement income is based on other sources. To determine their need, they have used a Monthly Income and Expense Worksheet (see figure 18), and, in the January column have listed their current income and expense situation as it exists today. In the February column, they have listed their income and expenses as they feel those would be should Allan become disabled. Note that the total expenses have dropped from $4,800 to $4,270; however, their income has dropped from $4,800 to $3,800. After subtracting income from expenses, they find they have a shortfall of $470. This is the amount of disability coverage they will need as a minimum to replace the lost earned income and to maintain the lifestyle they desire.

Some Basic Facts about Disability Insurance

While the needs for disability income insurance parallel those for life insurance, the contingency insured against is more difficult to define, and the considerations that must be weighed in determining disability can be highly subjective.

The insuring clause of a disability insurance contract gives the general definition of the coverage provided. It identifies the parties to the contract and states that insurance is provided for loss subject to all provisions, conditions, and exclusions of the policy.

Pre-existing conditions are excluded, subject to a statutory time limit, either in the insuring clause as cited above or through an appropriate definition of injury or sickness appearing elsewhere in the policy. A probationary period is included in some policies. It is usually applicable to sickness benefits, and requires that a loss occur more than 30 days after the policy date. This restriction has been removed from most new policies.

The definition of total disability, which is important in determining the liability of the insurer, is subject to variation. Early disability provisions of life insurance contracts and disability insurance policies provided for payment of lifetime benefits if the individual was unable to perform the duties of "his/her occupation." This led to abuse; some insured persons claimed total disability when they were unable to perform all duties of their occupation, even though their earning power was not substantially impaired. In 1929, the National Convention of Insurance Commissioners prohibited use of this definition in life insurance. Health insurance policies thereafter generally provided for a limited period of disability under "his/her occupation," followed by a definition defining total disability as "inability to perform the duties of any gainful occupation." A further modification of the gainful occupation definition resulted in addition of an additional phrase such as "for which he/she is reasonably fitted by education, training, and experience."

FIGURE 18   Monthly Income and Expense Worksheet

	INCOME	JAN	FEB	MAR	APR	MAY	JUN	JUL	AUG	SEP	OCT	NOV	DEC	TOTAL
1	Salary													
2	Salary—spouse													
3	Child support													
4	Alimony													
5	Dividend income													
6	Interest income													
7	Notes/loans receivable													
8	Mortgages receivable													
9	Trust income													
10	Pension income													
11	Other income													
12	TOTAL INCOME													

FIGURE 18   Monthly Income and Expense Worksheet   (continued)

EXPENSES	JAN	FEB	MAR	APR	MAY	JUN	JUL	AUG	SEP	OCT	NOV	DEC	TOTAL
1 Moving expense													
2 Employee business expense													
3 IRA													
4 IRA—spouse													
4 KEOGH													
6 KEOGH—spouse													
7 Interest penalties													
8 Alimony payments													
9 Federal income tax													
10 State income tax													
11 Local income tax													
12 Other withholdings													
13 Social security													
14 Property tax													
15 Charitable contributions													
16 Union dues													
17 Financial services													
18 Bank charges													
19 Rent													
20 Mortgage principal													
21 Mortgage interest													
22 Second home principal													
23 Second home interest													
24 Other interest													
TOTAL EXPENSES—THIS PAGE													

FIGURE 18   Monthly Income and Expense Worksheet   (continued)

EXPENSES	JAN	FEB	MAR	APR	MAY	JUN	JUL	AUG	SEP	OCT	NOV	DEC	TOTAL
25 Homeowner's insurance													
26 Auto insurance													
27 Health insurance													
28 Life insurance													
29 Disability insurance													
30 Liability insurance													
31 Other insurance													
32 Home repair													
33 Auto repair													
34 Auto expense													
35 Licenses													
36 Auto loans													
37 Other loans													
38 Other loans													
39 Charge cards													
40 Savings													
41 Investments													
42 Child support													
43 Child care													
44 Care for other dependents													
45 Domestic help													
46 Doctors													
47 Dentists													
TOTAL EXPENSES—THIS PAGE													

FIGURE 18 Monthly Income and Expense Worksheet (continued)

EXPENSES	JAN	FEB	MAR	APR	MAY	JUN	JUL	AUG	SEP	OCT	NOV	DEC	TOTAL
48 Medical—prescriptions													
49 Medical—other													
50 Electricity													
51 Gas													
52 Water/sewer													
53 Trash removal													
54 Miscellaneous utilities													
55 Telephone													
56 Gifts													
57 Food—at home													
58 Food—out													
59 Clothing													
60 Cleaning/laundry													
61 Personal care													
62 Pet care													
63 Entertainment													
64 Vacations													
65 Hobbies/recreation													
66 Books/magazines/newspapers													
67 Education													
68 Allowances													
69 Allownaces													
70 Appliances													
TOTAL EXPENSES—THIS PAGE													
TOTAL EXPENSES													

The trend in recent years has been toward liberalization of the period for which the "his/her occupation" definition is applicable. For the professions, currently the typical period allowed is for five or ten years, or to age 65. Shorter periods are offered applicants in occupational classes other than the professions.

Many contracts include partial disability benefits or offer the coverage as an option. The benefit is usually equal to the percentage of the total disability benefit. Partial disability often is defined as "the inability of the insured to perform one or more of the important duties of his/her occupation." This benefit is not particularly appropriate for employees (as differentiated from the self-employed) who normally return to full salary at the time of their return to work even though partially disabled. It is much more meaningful when applied to a self-employed individual who is dependent on his or her ability to perform all functions that relate to earnings.

The elimination period, that period of time at the inception of disability during which no benefits are payable, generally ranges from one week to one year, though in some exceptional situations a longer period such as two years may be provided when the insured person has adequate income protection for that length of time.

As the length of the elimination period increases, the cost of the premium subsequently payable decreases, making it possible for many individuals to secure protection against extended disability that otherwise would not be within their means.

The elimination period serves to avert some instances of overinsurance. It allows recognition of the economic circumstances and needs of the insured, without duplication through the programming of replacement income to supplement salary continuation programs, Social Security disability benefits, state cash sickness benefits, and group insurance short-term benefits.

The payment duration or benefit period of a policy will range from six months to the time the person reaches age 65, or even for the lifetime of the insured.

The vast majority of disabilities are of relatively short duration. Thus, policies with a short payment duration offer complete protection for most disabilities. However, they do not protect adequately against long-term disability, which is the most damaging economically. The length of the benefit period has a significant effect on the cost of the coverage, with the cost increasing as the benefit period lengthens.

A waiver-of-premium benefit is included in most individual disability income policies. The recent trend is to waive premiums throughout total disability, rather than during the benefit period only, and to return premiums paid during the qualification period.

For the insurance company, the amount of an applicant's earned income is the primary determinant in evaluating the amount of disability income. Net worth and unearned income are becoming of increasing concern; most companies consider these additional factors in connection with contracts providing larger benefits, and where there may be less incentive for an individual to return to work.

Each insurer establishes an issue limit, which is the maximum amount of disability income protection the company will provide for an individual, and a participation limit, which is the maximum total amount of coverage a person may have from all sources. Disability income benefits under a policy for which premiums are paid by the individual policyholder are tax-free. Therefore, benefits should be a limited percentage of earned income. Each company has its own formula for determining the percentage of a person's earned income that it will insure, usually grading down the percentage as earned income increases. Company issue and participation limits vary widely.

HEALTH INSURANCE

The major type of voluntary insurance in the United States is health insurance. It covers more persons, through more insurers, in more contract forms than life insurance.

The Social Security amendments of 1965, which included the Medicare program of health insurance for the elderly (see pages 169-197), were a significant landmark in the expansion by government into insuring against health losses. Some observers predicted that this legislation would mean the continual erosion of the health insurance market. However, today six out of ten persons 65 or older have private health insurance policies to supplement Medicare benefits.

Health insurance has as its purpose the payment of benefits for expenses arising from illness and injury. The loss of time from employment causes a loss of income to any working insured, and the cost of the medical care adds to the amount of that loss. Health insurance provides protection against the added expense of medical care.

Incapacity from illness or injury may cause a person to draw heavily upon savings to meet the costs of medical, nursing, or surgical care. Health insurance serves to protect savings by paying for current living expenses and making it unnecessary to sell the car or mortgage the home in order to pay heavy medical or surgical costs.

Major Types of Health Insurance

Two important types of insurance against the cost of medical care are hospital insurance (which includes protection against surgical and regular medical expense) and major medical expense protection.

Hospital.   Two objectives of hospital expense insurance are to help pay for the costs of hospital room and board and to help pay charges for hospital services. The policy limits the amount to be paid for each day of hospital confinement, and there is a limit with respect to the number of days that coverage applies.

The costs of specified operations are covered under surgical expenses. The protection includes surgery in a hospital, and it may include surgical procedures performed in the office or your home. Policies generally list the operations for which benefits are provided, together with a maximum amount payable for each. The schedule of operations generally includes all but the most unusual, and many insurers provide an equitable payment toward the cost of surgical procedures not specifically listed in the contracts. Not all policies covering hospitalization expenses include surgical benefits, but many do.

The regular medical expense form of insurance is designed to help pay doctors' fees for nonsurgical care in a hospital, at home, or at the physician's office. It is usually written as an optional coverage in conjunction with the basic hospital and surgical benefits. Some policies may provide preventive services, home nursing, X-ray treatment, laboratory and other diagnostic tests, and ambulance service, among other benefits.

Major Medical.   Major medical expense insurance provides coverage against catastrophic medical care costs. Instead of providing so-called first-dollar coverage, major medical insurance aims at paying only quite large medical losses. The usual hospital and surgical contracts provide for most medical expenses. There are, however, illnesses and injuries that are catastrophic; major operations, illnesses such as cancer and multiple sclerosis, and injuries resulting in total and permanent disability may subject a person or a family to expenses running into many thousands of dollars.

There are four identifying characteristics of major medical insurance: (1) the deductible, (2) participation or coinsurance, and (3) high maximum limits, and (4) blanket medical expenses.

The deductible feature obligates the insured person to pay the initial part of the expenses, which is called the deductible amount. For individual and family major medical policies, the common range of the deductible is between $100 and $1,000; it can go as high as $2,000. The purpose of the deductible is to avoid frequent small loss payments and thus keep the cost of the insurance low.

When expenses exceed the deductible amount, the policy benefits begin. Under a coinsurance feature (or participation agreement), the insurer then pays its share. For example, if the insurer is obligated to pay 80 percent of all hospital, doctor, and other medical bills in excess of the deductible sum, the remaining percentage, or 20 percent, is paid by the policyholder. The purpose of the coinsurance is to prevent overuse of or excessive costs for medical treatment.

Policy benefits are payable up to a maximum specified amount. Maximum benefit amounts of $500,000 or more are common today; unlimited amounts are also written. The maximum benefit may be written to apply to each illness or injury, or the benefit may limit the combined expenses for several injuries. Today's rapidly rising medical costs suggest frequent reevaluation of the limit carried.

All types of medical expenses are covered, on a blanket basis, including hospital, surgical, doctor, nursing, and miscellaneous medical costs. There are no individual limits that apply for the various types of expense.

The deductible and the coinsurance features operate together as follows: With a policy carrying a $500 deductible, in the event of a medical expense of $5,500, the insured pays the first $500 of expenses. With an 80 percent coinsurance feature, the insurer pays 80 percent of the balance ($5,000), or $4,000, and the insured pays $1,000. The total cost to the patient would be $1,500.

Many variations of the deductible and coinsurance features are used. The policy may provide that the deductible operate on a family basis and not on the basis of each individual illness. For example, in the case of a common accident or a contagious disease, the policy may provide for a common deductible. Some companies write a calendar deductible, which applies the deductible only once during the policy year. In the case of the per-illness or per-injury deductible, the cutoff is a maximum benefit limit applied within a period of two or three years.

Contracts offered by the various insurers vary greatly. Because there are many different forms of coverage and many differences among insurers, there tends to be much competition. Sometimes, emphasis is placed upon the protection afforded rather than upon the premium charged. If emphasis is placed upon a particularly low premium, the coverage under the contract may be expected to be limited. In this field, as in others, it is unreasonable to expect to get more than what is paid for. The policyholder should give careful attention to the details of the contract because failure to understand the limitations of the policy may lead to disappointment (see figure 19).

HOMEOWNER'S INSURANCE

Homeowner's, or residential, insurance compensates the insured to the extent of the actual cash value of property at the time of loss.

There are different forms of homeowner's insurance policies, and you should make sure to have the type that is right for you. In addition, there are many clauses, exclusions, and endorsements to contracts of insurance. Be sure you understand what you are and are not insured against. The worst time to find out you are not covered is when you have a claim.

Valuation of Property

Regardless of the policy amount, the loss payable is limited to the actual cash value of the property insured. The objective is repayment for the real loss sustained. The amount may be market value or book value, but often it is not. For many types of property, especially real estate, the actual cash value is equal to the replacement cost less depreciation. First, insurers figure the cost of replacing the property as new. They then subtract a reasonable estimate of actual depreciation due to age, use, and other factors, which have reduced the value of the property up to the time of loss. The depreciated amount is often much less than the book figures.

An exception to the rule of paying actual value is the replacement value coverage sometimes written to insure business buildings, and frequently to insure dwellings, for the full replacement cost (without deduction for depreciation) at the time of the loss. Under the policy terms, replacement value coverage is payable only if the property is rebuilt. Many homeowner's contracts today include this feature if the policyholder has at least 80 percent of the property value insured.

However, the basic contract does not undertake to supply "new for old." To do so could create a situation in which the insured might desire to have a loss in order to have new property in place of older property. Such a profit could increase the possibility of arson or fraud.

Depreciation includes the element of economic obsolescence. Thus, a property whose value is lessened by changing business conditions, neighborhood changes, and similar factors, is subject to depreciation when its value is computed for the purpose of loss adjustments. Actual cash value, which represents the the actual value of the property destroyed expressed

FIGURE 19   Checklist for Health Insurance

1. To ascertain the gaps in your overall health care coverage, check what you have or lack, and note whether what you have carries over into retirement.

Type of Health Care Insurance	*Do you have the coverage indicated?*		*If you are covered, will it carry over into retirement?*	
	Yes	No	Yes	No
• Blue Cross hospitalization	_____	_____	_____	_____
• Basic medical/surgical	_____	_____	_____	_____
• Comprehensive major medical	_____	_____	_____	_____
• Disability income medical	_____	_____	_____	_____
• Dental insurance	_____	_____	_____	_____
• Optical expense benefits	_____	_____	_____	_____
• Hearing aids	_____	_____	_____	_____
• Prescription drug plan	_____	_____	_____	_____
• Blood program	_____	_____	_____	_____

2. List the gaps in your present health insurance coverage: _____

_____

_____

3. List each health insurance coverage you have that will not carry over into retirement: _____

_____

_____

4. How do you plan to fill the gaps in your retirement health insurance package noted in your answers to questions 2 and 3 above?

_____

_____

_____

in terms of money, cannot be determined without giving consideration to depreciation of the physical property plus obsolescence.

Time and other factors frequently become an element in valuation. Many policies add the additional restriction, "but not exceeding the amount which it would cost to repair or replace the property with material of like kind and quality within a reasonable time after such loss, without allowance for any increased cost of repair or reconstruction by reason of any ordinance or law regulating construction or repair."

When the value exceeds the cost of repairing or replacing, the replacement cost becomes a limit on the amount recoverable. For example, a family moving to a rapidly growing community that is suffering a housing shortage might be willing to pay considerably more than replacement cost for immediate occupancy. However, this additional cost would not represent insurable value.

The clause limiting the loss to the cost to repair or replace is not an option to the insured; rather, it expresses a privilege granted to the insurer. It places an upper limit upon the cost, less depreciation, of repairing or replacing the materials that were damaged. The insurer seldom uses its option to repair or replace, since it is much easier to pay a cash amount than it is to replace or repair property.

Insurable Interest

It is the element of insurable interest that takes insurance out of the wagering classification and makes it a contract of indemnity. When the nature of an interest or liability in regard to property is such that the insured would lose financially if a loss occurs, an insurable interest exists.

The insuring clause limits the amount that may be recovered to the interest of the insured. Thus, insured persons may not collect for damages unless their interest in the property is such that the damage is actual loss to them. It is the intent of the policy to provide indemnity for loss sustained. A loss payment should not be made to persons who cannot show that they had a financial loss. For example, your neighbors cannot take out insurance on your home and collect for your loss.

Many different persons have insurable interests. Owners of property, mortgages, bailees, leaseholders, and some creditors are among the more common examples of persons having an insurable interest. Illustrations of the types of losses that can be insured, covering various insurable interests, are as follows:

- loss to buildings, whether the insured has a legal title, an equitable title, or beneficial ownership
- damage to, or loss of use of, personal property
- loss of income in the form of rent
- interest of a bailee in the use of property or the bailee's liability for its destruction
- interest of a person having a specific lien
- interest of a partner in partnership property
- liability of a transportation carrier to an owner
- interest of a leaseholder if the lease is terminated by fire damage
- improvements on leased property made by tenants
- interest of a mortgage
- interest of a large majority stockholder in corporate property

A mere expectancy without a definite legal basis is generally not insurable. A general creditor, therefore, has no insurable interest in the debtor's property unless a secured or specific lien such as a judgment lien has been acquired. A person named in a will as a recipient of property or a relative who may be an heir to an estate has no insurable interest prior to the death of the person holding the interest. To constitute insurable interest, the element of financial loss must be present. If the interest in a property is limited to a hope or an expectancy, there is no insurable interest.

There may be several insurable interests in the same property. Sometimes the loss check is payable to several parties, or "as their interests may appear." The sum of the insurable interests may exceed the total value of the property. Many of the interests described above can be concurrent. Also, insurable interests based on indirect loss to property or on liability are not limited to the value of the property. To make the extent of coverage clear, the insurable interest should be definitely stated in the policy.

Originally the requirement of an insurable interest was satisfied only if the interest in the property existed both at the time the policy was issued and at the time of the loss. Except in a few states, the doctrine now has been modified to recognize as valid a policy issued upon property in which an insurable interest did not exist at the time the policy was issued but was acquired later and was retained at the time the loss occurred. This rule validates a policy upon a stock of goods that is being increased or changed from time to time. Requiring an insurable interest only at the time of loss also permits coverage on goods in transportation where the insurable interest may not be present now but may come into being as title or responsibility for the goods changes.

Executors, trustees, and heirs are frequently concerned with the validity of insurance covering the property of the deceased. To make the coverage continuous, the standard contract states in the insuring agreement that the coverage remains effective for the insured's legal representatives in the event of the insured's death.

Coinsurance

The coinsurance clause aims at an equitable control of the amount of insurance that the insured shall carry. The purpose of the coinsurance clause is to provide equity among policyholders by encouraging them to carry a reasonable amount of insurance (usually 80 percent or more) in relating to the full value of their property. Although the coinsurance clause does not make mandatory the carrying of insurance up to a specified percentage of value, losses are adjusted as if insurance in such an amount were carried. Where there is a deficiency, the insured is said to be carrying that amount of risk and is, therefore, a coinsurer to the extent of the deficiency. The coinsurance clause is the simplest and fairest method devised to adjust charges and loss payments on the assumption that reasonable insurance amounts in relation to property values are carried. The insured should carry at least the percentage of insurance specified in the contract. Otherwise the insurer pays only part of the loss.

The application of the coinsurance clause may be expressed in the following formula:

Let

$$IC = \text{Insurance carried (the amount of insurance)}$$
$$IR = \text{Insurance required (the coinsurance percentage} \times \text{the value of the property at the time of loss)}$$
$$L = \text{Amount of the loss}$$

Then

$$\frac{IC}{IR} \times L = \text{Amount the insurer pays}$$

Suppose an insured purchased $60,000 of insurance from company X on a home valued at $100,000. If an 80 percent coinsurance clause was made a part of the contract and a loss of $40,000 occurred, the amount company X would be obligated to pay would be

$$\frac{\$60,000}{\$80,000} \times \$40,000, \text{ or } \frac{3}{4} \times \$40,000 = \$30,000$$

The insured would be a coinsurer to the extent of $10,000, since the property was not insured to 80 percent of the value. If the property was insured for $80,000, the loss would be paid in full by the insurer:

$$\frac{\$80,000}{\$80,000} \times \$40,000, \text{ or } 100\% \times \$40,000 = \$40,000$$

The second case, in which the insured carried the $80,000 as required by the coinsurance clause, illustrates the important principle that the insured is not just paid 80 percent of the loss when coinsurance is involved. The insured is paid the full loss amount (up to the amount of the policy) if at least the minimum required insurance amount is carried. The penalty applies only if the insured does not have at least the required amount. In the operation of the foregoing formula, the insurer is never liable for an amount in excess of the policies; hence, if the insurance was for $80,000 and the loss was $90,000, the insurer would be liable only for the $80,000 policy amount.

AUTOMOBILE INSURANCE

Many millions of automobiles, trucks, and buses are on the roads of America and each one is an individual problem for its owner or driver, as well as a source of possible costs and losses. Individual motorists solve many of these problems through the purchase of adequate automobile insurance coverages.

Three viewpoints are pertinent in appraising the need for automobile insurance: society, the automobile motorist, and the insured victims of automobile accidents. Automobile insurance is an individual solution to an individual problem of risk, but it also has social and public aspects. In the United States, there is almost universal acceptance of the idea that everyone owning or using an automobile should purchase liability insurance. The risk of financial disaster due to an automobile accident is so widespread that most persons need protection.

Types of Automobile Insurance

The two major coverages of automobile insurance are for casualty and for physical damages. The casualty coverages are bodily injury liability, property damage liability, medical payment, uninsured motorists, and, in some states, no-fault coverage. The physical damage category protects the insured from loss or damage to the car itself; this coverage includes fire, theft, collision, and a number of miscellaneous coverages such as windstorm, hail, earthquake, explosion, water damage, flood, riot and civil commotion, and vandalism and malicious mischief. The miscellaneous perils mentioned are often combined with fire and theft coverage in what is called comprehensive physical damage coverage.

Parts of the Automobile Insurance Contract

Basically, the parts of the auto insurance contract are as follows:
   Part A: Liability
   Part B: Medical payments
   Part C: Uninsured motorists
   Part D: Damage to your auto
   Part E: Duties after an accident or loss
   Part F: General provisions

Part A: Liability.

Bodily Injury and Property Damage.   The basic promise of the insurer in the liability portion is to *pay for bodily injury or property damage for which any covered person becomes legally responsible because of an accident.* Liability decisions aim at requiring those persons who are responsible for a loss to pay for it. Injury to other persons, including death, and damage to the property of other persons is included.

Single-limit Coverage.   One of the most significant changes in the personal auto policy is the single limit of coverage for both bodily injury and property damage. There were separate limits before in the family automobile policy, and bodily injury coverage had both a per-person and a per-occurrence limit. Now the single limit applies in any one auto accident, regardless of the number of covered persons, injured claimants, or property damage claims.

Defense and Supplementary Payments.   The insurer agrees to settle or defend any claim or suit asking for bodily injury or property damages because of an auto accident. This duty in the defense clause ends when the limit of liability has been exhausted. Settlement and defense costs include those of investigating claims, defense attorney fees, court costs, and other expenses of negotiation and defense.

   In addition to the policy limit, several supplementary payments are provided for.

Covered Persons.   One of the broadest features of the personal auto policy is that it protects more than just the named insured. The insurance applies to ownership, maintenance, or use of any auto or trailer by a covered person, defined in the contract to include, with respect to owned automobiles, the following:

- The named insured and spouse and any relative (including wards or foster children) living in the same household. This includes persons temporarily away from the household, such as children boarding at college.
- Any other person driving the insured's auto, if the driver can demonstrate that a reasonable belief that permission to use the auto exists (in previous policies, permission for use had to be given by the insured).
- Any person or organization, for liability arising out of any covered person's use of the covered auto on behalf of that person or organization (such as an employer).

With respect to nonowned automobiles, the policy also provides liability coverage for the following:

- Any person or organization, for the named insured's or family members' use of any auto or trailer, other than the covered auto or one owned by the person or organization. A common example is when the insured or members of the insured's family borrows or drives someone else's car (with reasonable belief of the right to use it). This coverage is often called drive-other-car coverage. It also provides protection to employers or organizations for other cars that may be used on their behalf by a covered person.

Exclusions.   The extension of coverage under the automobile contract to these categories of covered persons is seen as a very important part of the policy coverage. However, the coverage is limited by exclusions. Four exclusions pertain to the use of specific types of vehicles:

- Vehicles used in the auto business (selling, servicing, parking and so on).
- Trucks used in any other business or occupation (except covered autos), which may include pickup or panel trucks not customarily used in the insured's occupation or such trucks used similarly by farmers, ranchers, or federal employees.
- Vehicles with less than four wheels.
- Any vehicles while they are used to haul property or persons for a fee (except in shared-expense car pools, which are covered).

Also excluded is bodily injury to employees of the insured (except domestic employees if worker's compensation is not required). Another exclusion is coverage for property rented to, used by, or in the care of the insured (except damage to a nonowned residence or garage or damage to nonowned automobiles not furnished or available for the regular use of the named insured or family members). This means that vehicle damage to nonowned autos that are furnished or available for regular use is not covered. Only liability coverage for the named insured and spouse is provided in such cases. A final exclusion refers to a certain kind of wrongdoing by any person, for intentional bodily injury or property damage.

Policy Limits and Other Insurance.   The importance of the single limit of liability under the policy has been mentioned previously. Because all bodily injury and property damage claims come under the single limit, it is imperative for the policyholder to consider the purchase of as high a limit as is available and affordable. Although smaller standard limits (or those required by state laws) are purchaseable, few persons should consider less than a $50,000 limit, and most should buy coverage providing at least $100,000 or $300,000 liability limits. Most insurers will also quote the cost of even higher amounts, such as $500,000 or more, upon request.

Part B: Medical Payments.   The policyholder may include medical payments coverage in the personal automobile policy to cover the cost of medical services for the named insured, relatives, and anyone else in the insured's car. Part B does not apply to pedestrians or to occupants of buildings or other vehicles into which an insured vehicle may crash. This is really automobile accident insurance for medical care costs, and the protection applies without regard to whose fault the accident was. In effect, this is one of the original no-fault coverages and has been available in auto insurance for many years.

The advantage of having automobile medical payments coverage in addition to liability insurance is that payment is made promptly, without a wait for the determination of liability. This coverage also avoids many embarrassing or difficult claims or lawsuits by friends injured in your car, and it provides compensation for you and for members of your family, who are often unable to sustain a liability claim against you.

The coverage is quite broad, for all reasonable medical expenses (including surgical, dental, ambulance, hospital, and nursing) are paid, as well as funeral expenses, up to the policy limit. Injuries occurring in and upon entering or alighting from the automobile are covered. The high cost of medical services today makes the need for such protection obvious.

Part C: Uninsured Motorists. The recognition of the need for insurance to pay the insured, family members, and passengers for bodily injury caused by a negligent but uninsured motorist has led to the inclusion in the personal auto policy of protection against uninsured motorists. Increasingly popular since the early 1960s, the coverage is not mandatory in some states for every automobile insurance contract issued; in most states it is included in the contract unless the insured specifically rejects it in writing.

Coverage is usually now issued for a single limit of bodily injury liability as stated in the policy declarations. A limit similar to that of the basic liability coverage normally applies. By definition, an uninsured automobile is one that is not covered by a bodily injury liability policy or bond at the time of an accident. The definition is extended to include a hit-and-run automobile when the owner or operator of the car cannot be determined. It also includes other cars for which no insurance applies, such as stolen or improperly registered automobiles.

The insurance applies whether or not the injury caused by the uninsured motorist results from the occupancy of an automobile. The named insured and relatives are protected with insurance against accidents caused by uninsured motorists that occur when they occupy the owned automobile, operate bicycles, or are pedestrians. In any nonowned automobile operated by the named insured, only the named insured and relatives are covered.

Underinsured motorists coverage is also available, but only by an optional endorsement. It pays when the automobile bodily injury liability insurance carried by the negligent third party is exhausted.

Part D: Damage to Your Own Auto. Physical damage coverage for your own automobile is provided under Part D, if the declarations page indicates a premium charge and policy limit for the protection. This coverage should not be confused with property damage liability, which is the damage to the property of other persons for which you are held liable.

Part D may include all physical damage losses to your auto, or collision losses may be excluded if the collision peril is not shown in the declarations as covered and a premium charge is not indicated. Losses other than for collision are covered by a separate premium amount. Towing and labor costs for emergency road service up to $25 per disablement may be included in this part with an endorsement costing only a few dollars.

Physical damage insurance is related to the value of the automobile and to the need and ability of the owner to replace or repair the vehicle if it is damaged. Since most newer automobiles are items of large value in relation to the assets of a family, most owners need this insurance protection. However, as the value of an older car decreases, a time may be reached when physical damage insurance is not necessary to cover a possible maximum loss of a few hundred dollars. It is unwise to go without this coverage, however, if the value of the automobile is such that your income or assets could not readily replace the car if it is required for your work or family.

Sometimes you may have little choice as to whether you purchase physical damage insurance. Most installment contracts for the purchase of automobiles require that sufficient physical damage insurance be purchased to protect the value of the car as collateral. Two warnings are important in these cases: (1) the insurance that the bank or other creditor suggests or requires is usually limited to coverage on the car itself and should not be assumed to include the very important liability coverage or other automobile coverages; and (2) if the insurance cost is included in the finance plan, be sure to ask what coverages are included and to know the cost involved.

Collision Coverage.   Collision insurance reimburses you for damage to your automobile caused by a collision with another car with any other object, movable or fixed. The policy also specifically includes loss to the automobile caused by rolling over.

Collision insurance applies not only while the named insured is operating the automobile but also while other persons are operating it with a reasonable belief that they have the right to do so.

As with medical payments insurance, even if you do not carry collision insurance, you may be able to recover damages from the person who caused the accident. However, you would be wise to consider purchasing collision insurance for a number of reasons: You or the driver of your automobile may be responsible for the loss, whether or not another car is involved in the accident; if another party is responsible for the damage, you must prove negligence; and there may be delay and uncertainty in collecting from a negligent person (who may not have sufficient assets or insurance to pay the damages). If you carry collision insurance, regardless of whose fault the loss is, you will be paid for the damages to your car.

Collision losses are one of the most common situations in which subrogation may apply. That is, if you collect the damages from your insurer, the insurer may then take over your rights to sue the responsible party and recover the payment made to you. Whether the insurer will actually do so depends on many factors, including who was liable, the size of the loss, whether proof of negligence is readily available, and whether recovery of claims is likely from the other person.

Collision insurance is also a common illustration of the use of the deductible. The basic purpose of the deductible is to avoid the high cost and administrative expenses of frequent small collision losses.

The average collision deductible, which also applies to the comprehensive (other than collision) perils, provides that there shall be no liability on the part of the insurer unless the loss exceeds the named amount. Then the amount of the loss payment is only the amount of the loss that exceeds the deductible amount. For example, under a $100 deductible policy, if the loss is $90, there is no payment by the insurer; if the loss is $300, the insurer pays the policyholder $200.

Although the $50 deductible is still used in auto insurance, deductibles of $100 or more are being used with increasing frequency. The reduction in cost to you often justifies the decision to accept a larger portion of collision losses yourself. For example, if you can afford a $250 loss, and the reduction in premium for a $250 deductible as compared with a $100 deductible is $40, it may be unwise to have the smaller deductible. In effect, you may be paying a substantial premium for insurance you don't really need.

Ordinarily, you can expect to receive the deductible amount from the insurer if the insurer subrogates for the entire amount, including the deductible, and is successful in subrogation proceedings against another negligent party. The cost of the legal proceedings must be considered in a proportionate recovery. The insurer does not profit in subrogation cases and often recovers only a part of the payment it has made to you.

The insurer's limit of liability is usually for indemnity based upon the actual cash value of the automobile. The "actual cash value" wording protects the policyholder for losses on the basis of value as of the time of the loss, not exceeding the cost of repair or replacement. Other valid and collectible physical damage insurance of the insured on the automobile applies on a pro rata basis.

Comprehensive (Other than Collision) Coverage.   With the exception of collision losses, comprehensive physical damage is virtually an all-risk physical damage coverage. Protection is afforded for any direct and accidental loss of, or damage to, your automobile and its normal equipment.

Although the broad wording of the contract—"to pay for loss caused other than by collision to the owned automobile [used by an insured]"—would automatically include losses on an "everything but" basis, the clause does not give specific examples of the types of perils that are not considered to be collision losses.

To be covered, the damage must be accidental. It is not accidental damage if you break a window so that you can get into the car with the keys locked inside. The breakage of glass due to a collision is included as a covered comprehensive physical damage loss, but in a policy provision that applies only to glass breakage in a collision, the insured may choose to have it considered a collision loss. This avoids having a double deductible apply to glass breakage as both a collision and a comprehensive loss.

Another supplementary payment is provided in a clause that grants reimbursement for actual transportation expenses incurred following the theft of an automobile. This is a type of loss of use coverage.

Part E: Duties After an Accident or Loss.   The new and simplified wording of this part specifies what any person seeking coverage under the policy should do following an accident or loss. Many of the provisions are conditions that you as the insured must fulfill before you can expect the insurer to make payment under the contract.

Part F: General Provisions.   An assignment of the policy will not bind the insurer until it consents. To be valid, the assignment must be in writing and must be signed by an authorized officer of the insurer. Because of the nature of automobile coverages, the insurer wishes to underwrite its insured carefully. In the event of the named insured's death, the policy shall then cover the named insured's spouse, legal representatives in performing their duties, and anyone in temporary custody of the automobile.

Cancellation provisions require the insurer to give the policyholder ten days' notice in writing, with a proportional return (or offer to return) of unearned premium to the end of the policy period. If the insured cancels, the return of premium is calculated on the customary short-rate basis. Short rate includes an additional charge as a penalty for cancellation prior to premium due date. The personal automobile policy and many other automobile insurance contracts have recently limited the right of the insurer to cancel the liability portion of the coverage.

One provision in the policy incorporates the declarations into the agreement. The policy embraces all agreements relating to the insurance that exist between you and the insurer or any of its agents. Thus it is important that all material information called for appears in the declarations, since the contract is issued by the insurer in reliance upon their truth.

LIABILITY INSURANCE

"To sue or not to sue?"—that is the question! Situations involving injuries or damages are now regularly the basis for lawsuits by one person against another person or an organization. Many factors have contributed to the current litigious attacks in our society. Our ideas of individual, corporate, and social responsibilty have undergone many changes, and these changes have been reflected in increased reliance upon law to determine the extent of liability risk.

What emerges is an environment that places heavy emphasis on legal requirements and rights. Rarely can important decisions be made for family or business without considering their legal implications. A birth, a death, a marriage, a divorce, the purchase of a home, a new job, a new car, a sales contract, or the formation of a business enterprise—all of these have significant legal consequences.

Limiting Risk

For your protection you must learn to recognize negligence and other liability risk situations. Learning and applying risk-management techniques may be of help as the risks are analyzed and the methods of risk treatment considered.

Some liability situations can be controlled. You may choose not to own real estate or to lease an automobile or other equipment instead of owning it.

Some potential liability losses can be financed through risk-retention methods such as setting up a sound savings, reserve, or self-insurance plan. Some liability can be transferred to others, such as by hold-harmless agreements or other written contracts that make other persons responsible for part or all of liability losses.

However, several factors work against the exclusive reliance on these methods or risk reduction for liability situations. One is the complexity of the risk, based upon its legal nature, changing laws and interpretations, and the involvement of third parties (the claimant or injured person) in the legal liability process. Another is the large size of potential losses and the relative infrequency of loss. These characteristics make difficult the calculation of probabilities and variance of future losses, and they suggest the inability of many persons or firms to use risk retention as a sole method of liability risk management without the danger of serious financial expense from the larger losses.

Admittedly, some liability risks should be controlled by avoidance, prevention of losses, transfer by special contracts, but by far the likeliest choice for financing most of the liability losses is to transfer the risk by purchasing liability insurance.

Benefits of Liability Insurance

Liability insurance defends insured persons when claims are made against them, and settles with the claimants on reasonable terms if the insured persons are legally liable for the loss or damage. The liability insurance policy makes such payments as the insured persons would themselves have been obligated to pay because of the liability imposed by law. If there is no negligence on the part of the insured persons and hence no legal liability, there is no obligation on the part of the insurer to make any payment to a claimant. The insurer, however, is obligated to defend the insured against groundless claims, to bear the expenses thereof, and to make settlements subject to the limits of the policy in the event of unfavorable verdicts. In cases in which the question of liability is not clear, the insurer has the option to make a settlement, and frequently does. By so doing, the insurer saves the expense of litigation, and the insured is spared the inconvenience of a trial.

Types of Liability Policies

Two basic personal policies are the comprehensive personal liability policy and the farmers' comprehensive personal liability policy. The individual and the family need liability protection for numerous personal or individual situations. The ownership of residential property, participation in sports activities, the keeping of pets or animals, and many everyday activities all place a responsibility upon individuals not to cause injury or damage to other persons or their property.

Several other separate policies were used many years ago—a residence liability policy, a sports liability policy, and a dog liability policy—but now these coverages are almost always insured by the comprehensive personal policy instead.

In the liability insuring clause, the comprehensive personal liability policies, unlike most liability policies, cover under a single limit the liability of the insured for damage on account of bodily injury to members of the public and to employees, and for damage to the property of others caused by an occurrence. The single limit represents the maximum liability of the insurer regardless of the number of persons injured or the extent of property damage attributable to a single occurrence.

The comprehensive personal liability policy and the farmers' personal comprehensive liability policy are both designed to provide comprehensive liability protection for a named insured and the members of his or her household. However, certain perils in the farm risk are not found in the usual household, and the farmers' comprehensive policy is adapted to them. Although based primarily upon the personal liability exposures, the farmers' contract does include some business liability perils.

One of the most popular forms of excess liability insurance is the umbrella liability contract. The last 25 years have seen many variations of this policy. Many are nonstandard, and even those that follow a standard pattern have many important differences.

The umbrella liability contract is in excess in two respects: (1) it provides extra limits with a combined blanket single limit over other existing liability coverages, usually the required basic auto policy limits of $500,000 (as an example), a general liability contract for $100,000/$300,000/$100,000 limits, and employer's liability for $100,000; and (2) it is extra coverage for other liability exposures not covered by the underlying liability contracts, above a self-retention limit (the initial cost one is willing to pay). The maximum limit is high—at least $1 million, and often $5 million, $10 million, $20 million, or more.

These policies usually apply to the entire family and include residence, personal injury, automobile, employer's aircraft, sports, snowmobile, and watercraft liability. The usual exclusions include business pursuits or professional malpractice liability (both of which may be added by endorsement), property damage to aircraft, and nuclear energy liability. It is a recommended purchase for many persons because it helps meet the constantly changing large exposures to liability loss.

SELECTING AN INSURANCE PACKAGE

As you near retirement, insurance protection for yourself, your family, and your property takes on even greater importance. Life insurance needs should be reevaluated since health and accident problems generally accelerate in later years; likewise insurance protection for your home and possessions becomes increasingly necessary. A good insurance package should obviously offer adequate or better than adequate coverage. It should also offer you peace of mind and pass the worry on to the insurance carrier. It should be straightforward and easy to understand; nothing is more frustrating than dealing with confusing insurance clauses. It must be economical and cost-effective, offering coverage where you need it most and saving you money in areas where your need is not as great.

Here are some tips to keep in mind when selecting or reevaluating your insurance.

- Shop around and compare. Look for the package that offers the protection you need at the best price. Take the time to do some research.
- Avoid duplicate coverage. Buy just what you need to feel safe, and only what you can afford.
- Deal only with reputible insurance agents about whom you feel confident and comfortable.
- Beware of any major exclusions. Be sure all the risks you want covered are indeed part of the package.
- Make sure you have renewal rights. You must be able to hold on to the policy as you get older.
- Make sure you question any policies with maximum ceilings, especially if the payoff is low.

Don't let procrastination keep you from addressing these very important needs.

6

Estate Planning

Many people spend a considerable part of their lives in an attempt to accumulate enough property to enjoy retirement and, at death, provide for their loved ones. Estate planning encompasses the accumulation and disposition of property in a manner that allows the greatest possible fulfillment of these goals. When an individual no longer needs to use his or her entire income to provide for day-to-day living expenses, he or she must decide what types of property to acquire, how to handle that property, and when and how to dispose of it.

The primary goal of estate planning is to ensure the transfer of property to chosen beneficiaries at the smallest possible financial and emotional cost. Over a lifetime, a person can acquire several kinds of property and develop many personal relationships. The key elements of all estate plans are the assets comprising the estate and the characteristics of the intended beneficiaries.

Without an estate plan, heirs may incur unnecessary costs, and property may pass to individuals other than the desired beneficiaries. If the type of property that comprises the estate has not been properly integrated with the will in the form of ownership of estate assets, the estate plan will not accomplish its purpose.

Some results of an unplanned estate include the wrong beneficiaries inheriting the assets; the property being transferred in an unsuitable form; the property being tied up in trust when the circumstances at the time of death warrant outright distribution; children inheriting portions of a parent's estate, leaving the surviving spouse with insufficient funds; unnecessarily high estate taxes being incurred, which diminish the estate; unnecessary estate administration expenses being incurred; and a lack of liquidity, which may result in the forced sale of estate assets to raise money to pay taxes.

In addition to the normal trauma that accompanies a death, the survivors of the decedent, the person who has died, often experience intrafamily bitterness and reduced financial security. A properly planned estate reduces these problems and many times eliminates them.

"WHERE THERE'S A WILL...."

An up-to-date will, based on the circumstances existing at the death, should result in the orderly, sensible, and effective disposition of the decedent's property to the desired beneficiaries in the appropriate form.

A will also voids the application of local and testacy laws, which can require the outright distribution of portions of a deceased's estate to aging parents who may not need it or to children who may not be able to handle it, all to the detriment of the surviving spouse.

A will can also reduce the state administration costs by relieving the persons acting for the benefit of the decedent (the fiduciaries) of the necessity of obtaining costly bonds and by providing for guardians when necessary. In addition, a person's appointment of a competent executor, who is given proper powers, will facilitate the orderly administration of the estate and prevent potential disagreement, litigation, or both, about who should be the state's representative and how he or she should carry out the duties involved.

In addition to the will itself, a well-planned estate can achieve other significant benefits. An estate that contains a closely held business provides a good illustration of the importance of proper planning. Since the valuation of a small business is always difficult and usually leads to controversy and possible litigation, taxes and administrative costs can be saved if efforts to fix the value of the business are made prior to death. Also, when a small business constitutes a major asset of an estate, it is necessary to provide for liquid funds with which to pay the estate's taxes and administration expenses in order to avoid the necessity of a forced sale of the business itself. Another consideration should also be given to the qualification of the estate for the payment of the estate taxes in installments. The estate planner should consider predeath transfers of some of the estate owner's nonbusiness property to ensure that the business will constitute the required percentage of the value of the estate to qualify for installment payments.

Finally, estate planning can result in reducing the potential income taxes of the estate owner and the beneficiaries and the estate tax itself. Tax savings involves addressing the issues such as who should own what property, whether property should be owned jointly or separately, whether or when lifetime transfers should be made, whether a bequest should be outright or in a trust, and whether the fullest allowable marital deduction should be taken and how to be sure it will be allowed.

ELEMENTS OF THE ESTATE

The *estate* for purposes of estate planning consists of all the client's property. But the word *estate* can have different specific meanings depending on the modifying words that precede it.

The *probate estate* consists of those assets that will be transferred under the terms of the estate owner's will or that are subject to local intestacy law if there is no will. In general, probate property is property owned solely by the decedent that was not given away prior to death. The clearest way to define the probate estate is by discussing the types of property that are not part of it. All property that, on a decedent's death, passes "outside the will" is not part of the probate estate. Examples of such property are:

- life insurance proceeds paid to a designated beneficiary (other than the estate) who survives the decedent
- bank accounts, real estate or securities held in joint name with right of survivorship, where the other joint owner in fact survives
- bank accounts held in trust for someone who is living at the date of the decedent's death
- retirement plan or annuity contract benefits payable to a designated and surviving beneficiary
- property the decedent gave away, outright or in trust, during his or her life (even if the value of such property is subject to estate tax or is considered for purposes of estate tax computation)
- trusts created by others in which the decedent had an interest that is terminated by death, unless a general power of appointment was established that, in fact, was exercised in favor of the estate

The significance of the probate estate in the estate-planning process lies in the fact that only probate property is subject to the terms of the will. No matter how well a will is drafted to carry out an individual's wishes and to save taxes, unless there is an adequate amount of probate property, the will cannot accomplish its purposes. For example, if a will provides a specific cash bequest to a decedent's child, but all of the decedent's property consists of bank accounts, real estate, or securities held in joint name with the spouse, and the spouse is also designated as beneficiary of the decedent's life insurance, there is no probate estate out of which to pay the specific bequest. Another example involves an attempt to save estate taxes on the estate of a surviving spouse by providing in the will that a portion of the estate be held for the spouse in a trust, the value of which will not be included in the spouse's estate for estate tax purposes. If at death the person leaving the will does not own property in his or her own name and without predesignated beneficiaries, there will be no probate estate out of which to fund a testamentary trust. Usually, property held jointly with or in trust for a spouse will pass outright to the spouse and will be taxed in the spouse's estate. The same is true for life insurance and retirement plan death benefits if the spouse is designated as a beneficiary.

The *gross estate* refers to all of a decedent's property that is includable in the estate for estate-tax purposes. Also, the value of property given away by the decedent during his or her lifetime but to which he or she retained certain rights or powers is included in the gross estate. Property held in a decedent's name jointly with another is, generally, in the gross estate if the decedent paid for it; "in trust for" bank accounts and life insurance on the decedent's life is included in the gross estate if he or she retained incidents of ownership. Incidents of ownership are powers which, if retained by an individual, could mean the individual owns the policy even if they are not listed as owners.

The *adjusted gross estate* is the gross estate minus deductible funeral and administration expenses, claims against the estate, mortgages or indebtedness on property, the full value of which is included in the gross estate, and losses incurred during the settlement of the estate from fire, storms, other casualties, or theft to the extent not compensated for by insurance.

The *adjusted gross estate* is the figure upon which an estate's qualification is determined for capital gain treatment on the redemption of stock in a closely held business to pay estate taxes and administration expenses; it is also the figure that controls the qualification for the five-year deferral, with ten-year installment payment extension of time, for payment of estate taxes of estates containing closely held business interests.

The *taxable estate* is the adjusted gross estate minus any charitable, marital, and qualified sale of employer securities.

With the advent of the unified estate and gift tax concept and rate schedule, which applies to estates of persons who died after 1976, the value of the taxable estate alone determines the estate tax due only if the decedent made no taxable gifts after 1976. If such gifts were made, the amount of such gifts must be added to the amount of the taxable estate, and a tentative tax must be computed on such total under the unified estate and gift tax-rate schedule. This tentative tax is then reduced by gift taxes payable on the gifts given after 1976, to obtain the estate tax before the unified gift and estate tax credit, local and foreign death tax credits, and credit for tax on prior transfers are subtracted to arrive at the net estate tax payable.

MINIMIZING ESTATE TAXES AND COSTS

An important aspect of estate planning is the proper selection of the appropriate instruments and their use in a way that best provides for the desired dispositions to the beneficiaries at lowest tax and administration costs. A variety of instruments are available for achieving the goals of a given estate plan.

Gifts

The tax-related advantages to an estate owner of making lifetime gifts include the following:

- shifting the income earned by the donated property to a donee who is in a lower tax bracket
- increasing the size of the donee's estate, since $600,000 (for the estate of persons dying in 1987 and thereafter) may be transferred free of gift and/or estate tax as a result of the unified credit
- avoiding estate tax on any appreciation in value of the donated property occurring after the date of the gift
- eliminating from the donor's gross estate the amount of gift taxes paid on the gifts, but only if the donor lives for more than three years after the gift is made
- avoiding estate tax on all present interest gifts of $10,000 or less (other than gifts involving life insurance policies) made annually to separate donees

- enabling an estate that includes a closely held business to qualify for installment payments of estate tax, capital gains treatment for stock redemption, and special-use valuation of farms and other business realty by giving away assets other than the closely held business interest.

Consideration must be given to the applicability of the gift tax and to the unified gift and estate tax system, which applies to gifts made after 1976 and to the estates of persons who die after 1976.

The gift tax does not apply to annual present interest gifts of $10,000 or less per donee. Gifts to a donor's spouse are free of gift tax via the marital deduction. Charitable gifts, if in the proper form, are not subject to gift tax. All other gifts are taxable gifts, but the unified credit against gift and estate tax results in no gift tax due on gifts.

On the other hand, the value of all taxable gifts—those in excess of the annual $10,000 per donee exclusion and those not qualified for the marital or charitable deductions—will be added to the value of the estate owner's taxable estate for purposes of determining the estate tax due at death. And any gift tax paid on gifts made within the three years prior to the estate owner's death will be included in the gross estate. Also, the date-of-death value of any gifts over which the donor retains control, in the form of proscribed rights or powers, will be included in the gross estate.

Trusts

The two basic kinds of trust available are inter vivos trusts, those created by the estate owner during his or her life; and testamentary trusts, those created in the estate owner's will that come into being only upon death. A properly drawn trust with a competent trustee can offer its beneficiaries the benefits of property ownership without the usual burdens of property management.

Inter Vivos Trusts.   Inter vivos trusts provide professional property management for the beneficiary and can save income and/or estate taxes. For example, there is the housekeeping trust, which relieves the estate owner of the day-to-day management of property. Some persons—for example, a busy professional or executive, or a surviving spouse with little knowledge of property management—may derive significant benefits from placing some of their assets in trust. They can reserve the right to receive the income and, if needed, distributions from principal and the right to terminate the trust. They can select as trustee a person who, or bank that, will make investment decisions, clip coupons (send in coupons attached to coupon bonds in order to collect interest), deposit dividends, and prepare tax returns. This type of trust serves the estate-planning goal of permitting the estate owner to build an estate and enjoy its fruits without the usual burdens of investment choices and property management. However, the date-of-death value of any trust in which the grantor retains the beneficial interest will be included in the gross estate and be subject to estate tax. In addition, all the taxable income generated by the property trust is reportable by the grantor on the individual income-tax return. Thus, this kind of trust is not a tax-saving device.

Another class of inter vivos trust is the irrevocable trust for beneficiaries other than the grantor. If this type of trust is created, the estate owner usually gives up all rights to the property transferred to the trust. The basic difference between the creation of an inter vivos trust and an outright gift is that the inter vivos trust provides the beneficiary with competent property management and with protection from persons—including the beneficiaries—who might misuse or waste the gift. The value of property transferred to such trusts after 1976 constitutes part of the grantor's ultimate estate tax bracket if the transfer constitutes a taxable gift. Since outright gifts and irrevocable trusts differ only in terms of control over and protection of the beneficiary, the tax consequences are basically the same. The major benefits of the trust are that the income beneficiary of an irrevocable trust pays the income tax due on the property transferred to the trust; there will be no estate tax due on any appreciation in the value of the trust property after the transfer; and if the estate owner survives for three years after creating the trust, any gift tax actually paid on the creation of the trust is removed from the gross estate.

Some other kinds of inter vivos trusts sometimes used in the estate planning process are Code 2503(c) trusts for minors, which permit gifts to a minor to qualify as present interests for purposes of obtaining the annual gift tax exclusion, and trusts set up to receive the proceeds of the estate owner's life insurance or retirement plan death benefits, so that the proceeds can be held in trust for beneficiaries who ought not receive the proceeds outright for personal or tax reasons.

Testamentary Trusts.   The use of trusts in an estate owner's will depends upon the size of the estate and the personal characteristics of the intended beneficiaries. The size of the estate is important because the difficulties of administering small trusts outweigh their advantages. Also, corporate trustees will not handle small trusts, since their fees are based on the size of the trust. Assuming the estate is sufficiently substantial, trusts are used primarily to protect surviving spouses or minor children, and to save estate tax or reduce income tax.

Trusts for a surviving spouse are intended either to qualify for the marital deduction or to escape estate tax in the surviving spouse's estate. The primary reason for using a marital deduction trust instead of an outright bequest to the spouse is to relieve the spouse of property management decisions and chores. Trusts for a spouse, which are not intended to qualify for the marital deduction, can, if properly drawn, provide lifetime financial security for the spouse and can also escape inclusion in the spouse's estate for estate-tax purposes. Every estate is entitled to a credit that, in effect, permits the transfer of $600,000 free of estate tax. Significant overall estate tax savings can result by placing the amount of the exemption equivalent of the unified credit against estate tax available to the estate owner in a credit shelter trust. That amount will escape tax in both spouses' estates.

Trusts for children are valuable, since they provide for a qualified trustee, chosen by the estate owner, who can handle the property left to children in a manner permitting the greatest benefit to each child involved. Thus children's trusts can provide for distributing income and/or principal among the estate owner's children, according to their changing needs, until the youngest child has reached a specified age, or it can allow for fractions of the principal to be distributed at different ages.

Separate trusts for each child permit income-tax savings by dividing the taxable income among several taxpayers. But estate-tax savings, formerly obtainable by the creation of trusts to last for more than one generation of an estate owner's descendants, have been severely diminished by the generation-skipping tax. The $1 million exemption from this tax for each transferor does permit some estate-tax savings from long-term trusts.

Wills

The will is the most valuable instrument in estate planning (see figure 20). Among other things, a will can:

- provide a line of beneficiaries in the event that the primary beneficiary dies before the estate owner
- designate who should take various items of the probate property
- prescribe whether the property should be transferred outright or in trust, and, if in trust, whether income should be paid or accumulated; prescribe upon what events or criteria principal can be invaded; and

---

FIGURE 20   Basic Content of a Will

The basic content of a will includes the following:

1. place of residence: full address and state in which the will is drawn
2. statement revoking all previous wills
3. instructions for the payment of taxes, outstanding debts, costs of administration, and funeral and burial expenses
4. specific bequests: a listing of particular items to be given to specified individuals
5. general bequests: a listing of general sums to be given to specified individuals
6. bequests to charities
7. allocation of residual estate: a statement as to how the balance of the property is to be distributed
8. establishment of a trust or trusts, if any, and the naming of a trustee or trustees
9. naming of executor and guardian (if minor children are involved) and the powers of each

---

prescribe when outright distributions of part or all of the trust should occur
- coordinate the amount transferred to a spouse under the terms with property passing to the spouse outside the will, in order to qualify for the marital deduction and thus prevent unnecessary estate tax on the surviving spouse's estate
- provide which spouse shall be deemed to have survived in the event of simultaneous death
- designate the fund from which estate taxes are to be paid
- appoint guardians for children
- appoint executors and/or trustees
- provide the persons acting in behalf of the decedent with adequate powers to carry out the administration of estate taxes

In addition to a will, a Supplemental Letter of Instructions (see figure 21) is helpful to enable family members to facilitate personal and financial arrangements that must be made as soon after death as possible.

Also, Instructions for Funeral and Burial should be provided in detail (see figure 22).

FIGURE 21   Supplemental Letter of Instructions

	Name of husband or individual	Name of wife or individual
Legal name	_____	_____
Permanent address	_____	_____
	_____	_____
1. Persons to be notified of death		
(Name, address, phone number of each entry)	_____	_____
	_____	_____
	_____	_____
2. Location of original will	_____	_____
(Name, address, phone)		
	_____	_____
	_____	_____
Safe-deposit box	_____	_____
Lawyer	_____	_____
Bank trust department	_____	_____
Executor	_____	_____
3. Vital document information		
Birth certificate location	_____	_____
Birth date	_____	_____
Birthplace	_____	_____
Father's name	_____	_____
Mother's name	_____	_____
Marriage certificate location	_____	_____
Date married	_____	_____
Place married	_____	_____

FIGURE 21   Supplemental Letter of Instructions (continued)

	Name of husband or individual	*Name of wife or individual*
Prior marriages		
Names	_____	_____
Dates	_____	_____
How terminated	_____	_____
Veteran's discharge certificate		
Location	_____	_____
Service serial number	_____	_____
Date discharged	_____	_____
Place discharged	_____	_____
Social Security card location	_____	_____
Social Security number	_____	_____
Financial documents		
Location of paid bills	_____	_____
Location of past tax returns	_____	_____
Cancelled checks	_____	_____
4. Location of assets		
Safe-deposit boxes	_____	_____
Stock and bond certificates	_____	_____
Insurance policies	_____	_____
Pension documents	_____	_____
Bank accounts and bank books	_____	_____
Real property documents	_____	_____

FIGURE 21   Supplemental Letter of Instructions (concluded)

	Name of husband or individual	Name of wife or individual
5. My professional advisors		
(Name, address, phone)		
Lawyer	_____	_____
Accountant	_____	_____
Insurance agent	_____	_____
Broker	_____	_____
Bank or trust officer	_____	_____
Clergyperson	_____	_____
6. Employment/business data		
Present or last employer (indicate which)	_____	_____
(Name, address, phone)	_____	_____
	_____	_____
	_____	_____
Instructions re: business enterprise	_____	_____
	_____	_____
	_____	_____
	_____	_____
	_____	_____
	_____	_____
	(Signature)	(Signature)
	(Date)	(Date)

FIGURE 22   Instructions for Funeral and Burial

	Name of husband or individual	Name of wife or individual
1. Name, address, and phone number of funeral home selected	_____ _____ _____	_____ _____ _____
2. Type of service preferred		
At funeral facility	_____	_____
Church or synagogue	_____	_____
Name and address	_____	_____
Religious or nonreligious service	_____	_____
Private or public memorial service	_____	_____
Name of person to conduct service	_____	_____
Phone number	_____	_____
Names of speakers	_____	_____
Music	_____	_____
Flowers	_____	_____
Casket flag for a veteran	_____	_____
3. Casket		
Type and price range	_____	_____
Open for viewing or closed	_____	_____
4. Disposition of body		
Burial Earth burial or above ground in a mausoleum	_____	_____

FIGURE 22   Instructions for Funeral and Burial (concluded)

	Name of husband or individual	*Name of wife or individual*
Cremation		
Earth burial of urn, niche in columbarium, delivered to survivors, scattered on land or sea (specify)	_____	_____
Donation of body or parts. (Entire body or parts; list parts)	_____	_____
Name, address, and phone number of recipient organization (Attach authorization)	_____	_____
	_____	_____
	_____	_____
5. Name and location of cemetery	_____	_____
Individual grave or plot	_____	_____
Location of cemetery deed	_____	_____
6. Memorial contributions		
Name and address of charity or organization to receive memorial donations	_____	_____
7. Organizations to be notified		
Name of organization	_____	_____
Person to be contacted	_____	_____
Address and phone number	_____	_____
	_____	_____

Life Insurance

Life insurance is a unique tool in the estate-planning process. It is the only type of asset that can be used to create an estate to protect a young family in the period before a substantial estate is accumulated. Should the head of a young family die at a relatively young age, life insurance is worth many times what it has actually cost.

The other major advantage of life insurance is that it can provide a source of liquid funds, since it is usually paid soon after the insured's death. The proceeds are available to support the insured's family during the administration of the estate, and to pay debts and taxes, thus avoiding the forced sale of other estate assets.

There are two estate-planning considerations with respect to life insurance. First, should insurance on the estate owner's life be purchased and, if so, by whom? What kind of insurance? Who should pay the premiums? Who should be the designated beneficiary? Should the proceeds be taken in a lump sum or under an available settlement option? Second, if the estate owner's life is already insured, should ownership of some or all of the policies be transferred in an attempt to avoid the inclusion of the entire value of the proceeds in the gross estate? If the ownership of life insurance is transferred by the insured more than three years prior to death, and if the value of the transferred policy on the date of the gift is less than $10,000, the proceeds will neither be includable in the insured's gross estate nor will they push the insured's estate into higher tax brackets under the unified rate schedule, since gifts within the annual exclusion are not taxable gifts. If the date of gift value of the transferred policy exceeds $10,000, the amount of such excess is a taxable gift, unless the marital or charitable deductions apply, and the amount of the taxable gift will form part of the insured's ultimate estate tax bracket; the value of the proceeds, however, will escape estate-taxation. On the other hand, if the insured dies within three years after transferring his or her insurance, the entire value of the proceeds will be includable in the estate.

Retirement Plan Benefits

If the estate owner is employed, he or she may be a participant in a qualified employee retirement plan or may have an individual retirement account (IRA). A self-employed person may have a Keogh retirement plan or an IRA, or both.

In all cases, it must be decided to whom and in what form the retirement plan death benefits should be transferred at the estate owner's death. If the death benefit is paid to the decedent's surviving spouse, it will qualify for the marital deduction, thus avoiding estate tax liability in the decedent's estate. However, it will be subject to estate tax in the surviving spouse's estate. If the death benefits are made payable to the decedent's estate, they can provide liquid funds for the payment of debts and taxes.

Powers of Appointment

When a trust is created, the grantor (inter vivos trust) or testator (testamentary trust) dictates its terms. Tax considerations may require that an inter vivos trust be made irrevocable and its original terms not subject to amendment. The provisions of testamentary trusts are equally unalterable after the death of the person under whose will they are created. Since trusts often last for many years, the provisions made by the creator for the ultimate disposition of the trust property may be rendered inappropriate by events and changing circumstances that arise during the trust term. The estate-planning tool known as power of appointment provides a flexible solution. In its most common use, *power of appointment* refers to a right given by the creator to a beneficiary of the trust to name, either during the beneficiary's life or in the will, the ultimate recipients of the trust property. Only if the beneficiary does not exercise the power of appointment do the original provisions dictated by the trust's creator prevail. The beneficiary's power of appointment permits the original plan for the distribution of the trust's property to be altered in the light of circumstances that arise during the term of the trust.

There are two types of powers of appointment: General and special or limited. A general power of appointment gives the holder the right to appoint the property subject to his or her power to anyone at all, including the holder or the holder's estate. The value of the property over which a person has a general power of appointment is included in the gross estate of the holder at death.

A special power of appointment permits the holder to appoint among the persons designated by the creator of the trust, but in no event can the holder of the power appoint the property to the holder, the holder's creditors or the holder's estate. Because the holder of a special power cannot appoint to himself or herself, or his or her estate, the value of the property subject to the holder's power is not included in the holder's estate at his or her death.

Special powers of appointment may be given to a surviving spouse in qualified terminable interest property (Q/TIP) trusts, provided the power can only be exercised by the surviving spouse's will; or in credit shelter trusts, which consist of that part of the decedent spouse's estate that is not intended to qualify for the marital deduction because it is protected from tax by the unified credit. The surviving spouse is given the income of these trusts, and the trustees may have power to invade principal for the spouse's benefit under special, limited conditions. The balance of the trust at the spouse's death is usually divided equally among the decedent's then-living successors unless the spouse exercises his or her special power of appointment to benefit those among the decedent's successors who have the most need. Thus, if, after the death of the descendent's spouse, one of the children is widowed, goes bankrupt, or is subject to a serious illness or accident, the surviving spouse can exercise power of appointment to alter the distribution of trust principal at his or her death so that the one to whom the misfortune occurred receives more than the others—or even the entire principal if that is warranted. The special power of appointment thus permits a limited amount of postmortem estate planning for the decedent's family.

Disclaimers and Elective Bequests. Another estate-planning tool that permits some postmortem flexibility is the disclaimer and the closely related elective bequest. The major purpose here is to reduce estate taxes. A disclaimer or renunciation is the refusal to accept all or a portion of an intestate share of the estate of a decedent who dies without a valid will or a bequest under a valid will. A qualified disclaimer has the effect for tax purposes of treating the disclaimed interest as if it had never been transferred to the disclaimant. Thus the disclaimed interest never becomes part of the disclaimant's gross estate, nor is the descendent deemed to have made a gift to the person to whom the disclaimed interest passes. To be a qualified disclaimer, the disclaimer must be made within nine months after the interest being disclaimed was created, it must be in writing, and as a result of the disclaimer the property must pass to the decedent's spouse or to someone other than the disclaimant. A timely made written transfer is also treated as a qualified disclaimer to the persons who would have benefitted if an effective disclaimer could have been made.

Disclaimers can be used to save estate taxes both during the estate owner's life and after his or her death. If, for example, the estate owner becomes entitled to an intestate share of a relative's estate or to a bequest under someone's will and accepts the property, his or her own estate will be increased by its value. If, however, the estate owner disclaims the interest, he or she not only avoids the additional tax on his or her own estate, but the disclaimed interest will often pass, by the intestacy laws or by the terms of the will, to the estate owner's own descendants, who are usually the intended beneficiaries. Thus, the disclaimer can result in the passage of property to the estate owner's beneficiaries free of any gift or estate tax.

Closely related to the disclaimer is the will provision for an elective bequest. Here, the spouse is given enough property to qualify for the fullest marital deduction. However, he or she is required by the will to elect to accept or reject the bequest, in whole or in part, within six months after the death of the spouse leaving the will (the testator). Another form of elective bequest is a will provision that gives the spouse a life estate in certain property interests but permits the spouse to elect, within six months, to take the property outright. Both of these elective bequest provisions have been held to qualify for the marital deduction whether the spouse accepted the bequest or elected to take it outright. If, however, at the time of the testator's death, the estate does not exceed the amount protected from tax by the unified credit available to the estate, or the surviving spouse has a substantial estate of his or her own, rejection of all or part of the marital deduction bequest, or taking only a life estate (the property interest defined by the duration of that persons' life), can result in lower estate taxes on the combined estates of both spouses, thus leaving more for the children.

Qualified Terminable Interest Property (Q/TIP) Bequests.   Postmortem flexibility can be obtained by the use of qualified terminable interest property (Q/TIP) bequests in the form of a trust under which the surviving spouse is entitled to all the income for life, and no person can appoint any part of the property to anyone other than the surviving spouse during his or her lifetime. If a bequest is made to a surviving spouse in the form of a Q/TIP trust, the marital deduction is available for the trust property only if the executor of the estate owner's estate elects to claim it. If the marital deduction election is made, the trust property will be subject to gift tax if the surviving spouse disposes of all or part of the income interest during his or her lifetime, or subject to estate tax on the surviving spouse's death.

For planning purposes, the Q/TIP trust gives the estate owner's executor a choice after the estate owner's death. The executor can elect to take the marital deduction for the trust property (not just the spouse's income interest) and therefore defer estate tax until the surviving spouse's death (unless the executor makes a prior gift, in which case a gift tax will be payable). Conversely, the executor can elect not to take the marital deduction for the trust property, and cause it to be subject to estate tax in the estate owner's estate but not subject to gift or state tax on subsequent disposition by the surviving spouse during his or her lifetime or upon death.

This is the choice given to the executor: Qualifying the Q/TIP trust property for the marital deduction and deferring estate tax, or not qualifying it for the marital deduction and exposing it to tax at the estate owner's death. The alternatives provide the Q/TIP trust with its unique estate-planning advantages, since the choice can be made after the estate owner's death, based on the situation as it exists at that time.

PLANNING THE ESTATE

Estate planning is primarily a legal transaction since the plan will be effected by one or more legal documents, the most prominent of which is the will itself. Lawyers, therefore, usually coordinate the estate-planning process.

In many cases, however, estate planning involves much more than the drafting of wills and other legal documents. In such cases, the concept of the estate-planning team comes into play. The other team members, in appropriate cases, are the accountant, the bank trust officer, the insurance advisor, the investment counselor, and the financial planner.

All of these advisors play vital roles in the estate-planning process and should be consulted prior to and during the creation and implementation of your estate plan. Before meeting with them to discuss your desires, you may find it useful to complete a financial statement (see figure 15) and the information for Estate-Planning Conference Worksheet (see figure 23).

These will be extremely helpful aids in obtaining the information necessary to formulate the estate plan. They are designed to elicit information pertinent to preparation of the plan, and to record such information so that it is readily available for reference at all times during the estate-planning process and thereafter.

How Federal Taxation Affects the Estate Plan

The principal objective of an estate plan is to provide an arrangement for the orderly disposition of the estate owner's assets in accordance with his or her wishes. A secondary, though important, objective of the plan is to provide an arrangement for dispositions that will keep income and death taxes at a minimum and, if the plan calls for lifetime gifts, to minimize gift taxes on the estate and its beneficiaries (income tax), on the transfer of assets during a lifetime (gift tax and in some cases estate tax and

FIGURE 23   Information for Estate-Planning Conference Worksheet

FAMILY INFORMATION

Date: _____

Full legal name _____

Address and phone number _____

Birth date _____ Social Security number _____

Employers (last 10 years)

_____

_____

_____

Veteran? _____ Service No. _____

Disability: Service-connected or nonservice-connected _____

Marital status: single, married, widowed, separated, or divorced

Do you have a will? _____

Legal name of spouse _____

Address and phone number _____

Birth date _____ Social Security number _____

Does spouse have a will? _____

Children, including those legally adopted:

Full name	Full address	Birth date	Extent of dependence
_____	_____	_____	_____
_____	_____	_____	_____

FIGURE 23 Information for Estate-Planning Conference Worksheet (continued)

Other dependents:

Full name	**Full address**	**Birth date**	**Extent of dependence**
_____	_____	_____	_____
_____	_____	_____	_____

Annual income: Salary _____ Investment income _____

BENEFICIARY INFORMATION

Names of individuals or charities	**Bequest: Dollars or percent of estate**
_____	_____
_____	_____
_____	_____

EXECUTOR, GUARDIAN, TRUSTEE INFORMATION

(1) The following person and/or bank trust department should be executor of my estate:

Name and address of person and/or bank _____

Name and address of alternate executor _____

(2) The following person(s) should be the guardian(s) of my children:

Name and address _____

Name and address of alternate _____

(3) The following person and/or bank trust department should be the trustee for any trust that may be established:

Name and address _____

Name and address of alternate _____

FIGURE 23   Information for Estate-Planning Conference Worksheet (concluded)

PROPERTY INFORMATION

Real estate:

Description and location	Market value	In name(s) of	Amount of mortgage
_____	_____	_____	_____
_____	_____	_____	_____
_____	_____	_____	_____

Leases: _____

Bank accounts: _____

Stocks and bonds: _____

Other assets: _____

Pension benefits: _____

_____

Insurance:

Name of company	Policy number	Beneficiary or owner	Amount of policy
_____	_____	_____	_____
_____	_____	_____	_____
_____	_____	_____	_____

generation-skipping tax) and on the transfer of assets at or after death (estate tax or generation-skipping tax).

The federal estate tax is in general imposed on the transfer of the estate owner's assets at death, but it is imposed also on certain lifetime transfers considered to be testamentary in character. It is based on the value of the gross estate, which includes all property and property interests owned by the decedent at death, testamentary-type lifetime transfers, and certain other property and property interests, such as property subject to taxable powers of appointment, property owned by the estate owner jointly with others, and certain employee benefits. Deductions from the gross estate allowed in computing the taxable estate include funeral and administration expenses, certain losses to the estate during administration, the marital deduction, and charitable deductions.

In preparing an estate plan, it is usually desirable to arrange for dispositions of the estate owner's assets that minimize the federal estate tax imposed on the estate owner's estate, as well as estate taxes imposed on the estate of any surviving spouse, and in certain situations, on the estates of other beneficiaries such as children and grandchildren. In designing a plan to achieve federal estate-tax savings, however, it is necessary to guard against distortion of the most desirable features of the plan for distributions.

Minimization of federal estate taxes under an estate plan is generally achieved by making dispositions that

* remove assets from the estate owner's gross estate through lifetime gifts
* remove assets from the estate owner's taxable estate
* avoid inclusion of assets in the gross estate of a beneficiary of the estate owner's estate

Effect of Federal Estate Taxes on the Form of Ownership of Property.   The form of ownership of property can be significantly affected by federal estate taxes, with the result that the estate plan may call for a change in the existing form of ownership. For example, the federal estate-tax consequences of owning property separately can be far different than the tax consequences of owning property jointly with one or more other persons. Even among the various types of joint ownership of property, there are significant variations in the federal estate-tax consequences.

Limitations on the Estate Plan

Although estate owners are, for the most part, free to dispose of their assets as they wish, there are some limitations imposed by law or by individual circumstances.

Surviving Spouse's Rights.   A married estate owner must make provisions for a surviving spouse under the law of almost every state. Failure to give at least the minimum amount required by the law—the domicile—results in the right of the surviving spouse to take a statutory share of the estate outright. This "right of election" can upset a carefully prepared testamentary plan, since the property subject to the terms of the will is reduced by the amount of the spouse's elective share.

Most of the community property states do not have provisions for election against the will, since the spouse is deemed to be adequately protected by community property rights. Community property is a form of ownership where property is owned equally by both parties.

State laws vary considerably in what a surviving spouse is entitled to. Some states limit the survivor's rights to dower or curtesy, which usually consists of a life estate in part or all of the deceased spouse's real estate holdings. Other states permit the survivor to take one-third of the decedent's estate if there are children surviving or one-half of the estate if there are no children. The estate for purposes of the election may be the probate estate; the net estate after all or some of the enforceable claims against the estate are deducted; or the augmented estate, which includes the probate estate plus part or all of the value of inter vivos gifts made by the decedent to someone other than the spouse, and property held by the decedent and someone other than the spouse as joint tenants that passes to the other tenant or tenants upon the decedent's death. Still other states permit the surviving spouse to elect the intestate share—that is, what the spouse would have received had the decedent died without a will.

A spouse's right of election can usually be waived by antenuptial agreement and is usually terminated by the final decree and agreement of an absolute divorce.

Rights of Children.   Children may be disinherited under the laws of almost every state. However, in some states, it is necessary that the will make clear that the disinheritance is intentional, rather than due to mistake, particularly if the omitted child was born or adopted after the execution of the will. Thus, the laws of many states provide that a child born or adopted after the execution of a parent's will is entitled to an intestate share if no provision is made for the child in the will, and the child has not received a share of the parent's estate by inter vivos gifts. This right can be defeated only if the will makes it clear that the failure to provide for the child was intentional. In some states, the fact that the testator (the person making the will) had one or more children living when the will was executed and gave most or all of the estate to the other parent of the omitted afterborn child is deemed to be adequate evidence that the omission of all the children, including those born or adopted after the will was executed, was intentional.

In those states that permit children—born before the will was executed and not provided for in the will—to take an intestate share of the parent's estate, evidence that the failure to provide for such children was intentional will defeat children's right to take such a share.

Rule Against Perpetuities.   The common law rule against perpetuities provides that interests in a trust must vest or obtain rights of ownership within a period limited to lives-in-being plus 21 years plus a period of gestation. The majority of states have adopted the common law rule, either by statute or under case law.

A fairly frequent example of the limitation that this rule imposes on an estate plan occurs when a testator puts property in trust for the life of a spouse and directs that at the spouse's death the property is to be divided into shares for the then-living children and for the then-living children of any child or children who are not then living. Since the children of the testator were in being at the time of death, the rule is not violated if the testator directs that the property be held in trust for the lifetime of his or her child. However, any share set apart for the issue of a predeceased child (a child that dies before inheritance) cannot be held in trust for the life of such children without the risk of violating the rule, since they may have been born after the testator's death (during the life of the surviving spouse). Thus the will must provide that any share being held in trust for children born after the death of the testator must terminate no later than 21 years after the death of specified persons who were in being at the date of the testator's death. For example, the will can direct that a trust for children not in being at the time of the testator's death shall terminate, and the principal shall be paid over to such children, at the expiration of 21 years following the death of the last survivor of the testator's children who was living at the time of death.

Restrictions on Period of Income Accumulation.   In the great majority of states, income may be accumulated in a trust for the same length of time that the trust may last under the rule against perpetuities. A few states still restrict the permissible period for income accumulation to the age of minority of the trust beneficiary who was living when the trust was created.

THE ALTERNATIVES TO PLANNING

Formal estate-planning includes the execution of a will and often involves the creating of inter vivos trusts, making gifts, creating employee-benefit plans, arranging for the valuation and disposition of a closely held business interest, and so on. One or more professional estate-planning advisors are employed in the task of accomplishing the best possible result. The two alternatives to formal planning are no planning (intestacy) and informal planning by the estate owner himself.

Intestacy

Intestacy, which is the legal term for death without a valid will, results in the intestate decedent's estate plan being created by the laws of the state in which he or she had a principal residence at the time of death. These laws provide for the distribution of property owned by someone who dies without a valid will and without having chosen beneficiaries either by means of the form in which the property was owned or by contract. An example of a contract might be the insurance policy or employee-benefit plan under which the decedent was able to designate beneficiaries and the form and amount of their shares).

State intestate-distribution statutes follow the general pattern of distributing the intestate's estate to the closest surviving relatives. But the amounts to which each relative is entitled and the degrees of relationship to which the testacy law extends vary from state to state.

Intestacy laws are rigid and objective. They deal only with the degrees of relationship and not with the individual circumstances of each owner's family situation.

Some of the problems inherent in permitting property to pass by intestacy are as follows:

1. People whom the estate owner might wish to benefit but who are not legally related will take nothing.
2. The beneficiaries take their shares outright, regardless of their age or ability to handle property.

3. When the beneficiaries are minors, guardians must be appointed to handle the property. The choice of the guardian lies with the local court, and the guardian's fees must be paid out of estate assets.
4. A surviving spouse will usually not receive an adequate share of the estate if there are children surviving, since at least half the estate will go to the children.
5. The amount passing to a surviving spouse as his or her intestate share often will not be enough to take full advantage of the federal estate-tax marital deduction.
6. Estate taxes that could have been avoided may be due. This will happen where full use of the marital deduction might have avoided estate tax, but the shares passing to the children under the intestacy laws exceed the amount protected from federal estate tax by the unified credit.
7. Additional estate-administration expenses will be incurred. Examples are fiduciary's bonds and guardian's fee, which might have been eliminated by appropriate provisions in a will.
8. The person appointed to administer the decedent's estate will be chosen by the court, and the choice will be based primarily on the degree of familial relationship to the decedent and not on the competence of the person to handle the administration of the estate.
9. If the decedent leaves minor children and no spouse, the choice of the children's guardian rests with the court and often results in litigation concerning who is best qualified to care for the children—a result that often is not in the best interests of the children.
10. The powers of the chosen fiduciary to handle the property left by the intestate decedent are restricted to those granted under state law, and the fiduciary must often seek permission from the court before he or she can act. This results in delay, which can be costly to the estate, and in additional administration expenses.

Pattern of Intestate Distribution.   While local laws vary to some degree, the distribution of an intestate decedent's property follows this general pattern if the decedent is survived by:

- A spouse and one child—The spouse receives one-half; the child gets the balance. In some states, the spouse is entitled to a specified dollar amount, often $25,000 or $50,000, in addition to his or her percentage.
- A spouse and children—One-third goes to the spouse, the balance to the children equally, or their issue per stirpes (children of a deceased

child) take the share to which their parent would have been entitled).
The spouse may receive a specific dollar amount in addition to his or
her percentage.

- No spouse, but with children—The entire estate goes to the children
  equally, or their issue stirpes.
- Spouse and no children—The spouse usually receives a specific dollar
  amount plus one-half of the balance, with the other half going to the
  decedent's parents. If no parent survives, the spouse takes the entire
  estate. In a few states, the spouse receives the entire estate even if the
  decedent leaves a surviving parent.
- No spouse, no children—The entire estate goes to the parents equally,
  or to the surviving parent. If no parent survives, all goes to brothers
  and sisters or their issue per stirpes, and if none, to grandparents or
  their issue.

A few states treat the intestate's real and personal property differently, sometimes giving a surviving spouse only a life estate in part of all
of the decedent's real estate. This gives the surviving spouse property interest only during his or her life.

Joint and Other Special Forms of Ownership

An estate owner can try to plan the distribution of some types of property at his or her death by having title to the property registered in the estate owner's name and the names of intended beneficiaries as joint owners
with rights of survivorship.

The distribution of other types of assets, particularly life insurance
and death benefits under employee-benefit plans, at the estate owner's
death can be preplanned by the designation of beneficiaries to take the
proceeds and benefits upon the estate owner's death. The amount and
method of payment, lump-sum or partial payments over a period of
time, can also be designated under the policy or plan.

Savings accounts can be held in trust for a designated beneficiary and
will pass to that person at the estate owner's death.

The above methods of directing the transference of property at death
are certainly useful, but they do not, as is sometimes claimed, obviate the
need for a will or for comprehensive estate planning by professionals.
Some of the shortcomings of planning through joint and other special
forms of ownership are:

1. Some types of assets generally are not covered by this kind of planning. Examples of such property are household furnishings; stamp,

coin, and art collections; furs, jewelry, china, silver, and other tangible personal property; partnership interests; businesses conducted in unincorporated form; professional practices; copyrights; patents; and claims under medical insurance policies or wrongful death statutes.

2. If property is held jointly with or in trust for someone, problems arise if the estate owner and the other joint owner or the designated beneficiary die simultaneously. The Uniform Simultaneous Death Act, which has been adopted in most states, provides that where two joint tenants or tenants by the entirety, (a joint tenancy requiring both parties' consent) die simultaneously, the property so held shall be distributed one-half as if one of the joint tenants had survived, and one-half as if the other had survived. If one or both joint tenants die without wills, the jointly owned property will be distributed to the intestate beneficiaries of both owners.

   The act provides with respect to life and accident insurance that if the insured and the beneficiary die simultaneously, the insured shall be considered to have survived the beneficiary. Thus, if only one beneficiary is named, and that beneficiary and the insured die simultaneously, the proceeds will be payable to the insured's estate. If the insured has no will, the proceeds will pass to those entitled under the state intestacy statutes.

   Except as otherwise provided for joint tenants and others, whenever one person's right to take another person's property depends upon the former surviving, if the two die simultaneously, the person who owned the property is deemed to have survived. Thus, if A and B die at the same time, a bank account registered in A's name in trust for B will be distributed as if A had survived.

3. If the person designated as joint owner dies before the estate owner, the property belongs solely to the estate owner as survivor. If the estate owner has no will, the property will pass by intestacy unless the estate owner reregisters the property and names the next intended beneficiary as joint owner. The same problem exists if a designated beneficiary for life insurance or employee-plan benefits dies before the insured (or employee), unless a successor beneficiary was named.

4. Property held as joint tenants or tenants by the entirety and bank accounts owned in trust for a designated beneficiary pass outright at the estate owner's death to the other tenant or the beneficiary if he or she survives. Passage of property in outright form can create both personal and tax problems. Thus, the property so owned cannot be held in trust for a beneficiary who is incapable of managing

property due to lack of experience or immature or advanced age. In addition, the *income* and *remainder* (the amount left over after taxes) interests in such property cannot be split by the estate owner to benefit more than one person.

Tax problems may be caused by joint and other special forms of ownership. When the joint tenants are husband and wife, one-half the value of the property will be included in the estate of the first spouse to die, and only that half will receive *a basis equal to its value in the decedent spouse's estate*. If the property has appreciated substantially since the spouses acquired it, failure to obtain a stepped-up basis for the other half of the jointly owned property can result in unnecessary income tax liability on the sale of the property by the surviving spouse.

The value of such property may be taxed in the estates of both joint tenants. This latter problem occurs when the joint tenants are not spouses. Thus, if a brother and sister or parent and child hold property jointly, the entire value of such property will be includable in the estate of the first to die (unless the survivor can prove his or her contribution), and then in the estate of the survivor if he or she still owns the property at his or her death. The only partial relief might be the credit for estate tax on prior transfers, which is available only if the survivor dies within ten years after the death of the first joint tenant to die.

Another tax problem that occurs when an estate owner attempts to plan the disposition of the estate by joint ownership and beneficiary designations in lieu of a will is the necessity of collecting the estate taxes due from the person to whom the property passes. In most states, unless an estate owner directs otherwise, the estate tax due must be apportioned against and paid by the recipients of the property. Since beneficiaries often do not expect to have to pay tax on inherited property, collecting the estate tax from them can be difficult for the administrator of the estate.

QUESTIONS TO ASK ABOUT YOUR ESTATE PLAN

When done properly, estate planning can assure you that the assets you have worked all your life to accumulate are passed to the proper people in the proper manner. Make sure that you have addressed the following questions in your estate plan:

1. Will your surviving family have enough cash to pay ordinary family living expenses while the estate is in probate?
2. Do you have special directions for the funeral, disposition of your body, or memorials?

3. How do you wish to dispose of tangible personal property?
4. Do you wish to make any specific bequests or legacies?
5. Do you wish to dispose of real property?
6. Do you wish to provide for periodic payments of income for certain beneficiaries?
7. What arrangements do you wish to make for minor children or incompetent adult beneficiaries?
8. Do you want to establish trusts for certain beneficiaries, or do you want them to receive the assets outright?
9. What provisions should be made to dispose of your business interests?
10. How should federal estate taxes and state death taxes, if any, be paid out of the estate?
11. Should any special powers be given to or taken away from the executor?
12. Who should serve as executor, trustee, or guardian?

When thought through and carefully answered, these questions will provide you with a helpful guideline in achieving your estate planning objectives.

A LIVING WILL

Many persons are opting to include a living will in plans for their future. In essence, the will requests that the individual not be kept alive by heroic measures if there is no reasonable expectation of recovery. See figure 24 for a copy of a living will and directions for preparing one.

FIGURE 24   A Living Will

To my family, my physician, my lawyer, my clergyperson; to any medical facility in whose care I happen to be; to any individual who may become responsible for my health, welfare, or affairs:

Death is as much a reality as birth, growth, maturity, and old age—it is the one certainty of life. If the time comes when I, _____ , can no longer take part in decisions for my own future, let this statement stand as an expression of my wishes, while I am still of sound mind.

If the situation should arise in which there is no reasonable expectation of my recovery from physical or mental disability, I request that I be allowed to die and not be kept alive by artificial means or "heroic measures." I do not fear death itself as much as the indignities of deterioration, dependence, and hopeless pain. I, therefore, ask that medication be mercifully administered to me to alleviate suffering even though this may hasten the moment of death.

This request is made after careful consideration. I hope you who care for me will feel morally bound to follow its mandate. I recognize that this appears to place a heavy responsibility upon you, but it is with the intention of relieving you of such a responsibility and of placing it upon myself in accordance with my strong convictions, that this statement is made.

Date _____   Signed _____

Witness _____   Witness _____

Copies of this request have been given to _____

_____

_____

Directions for the Living Will

1. Sign and date before two witnesses. (This is to insure that you signed of your own free will and not under any pressure.)

2. If you have a doctor, provide a copy for your medical file and discuss the will with him or her to make sure the doctor is in agreement. Also give copies to those most likely to be concerned if the time comes when you can no longer take part in decisions for your own future. Enter their names on the bottom lines of the Living Will. Keep the original nearby, easily and readily available.

3. Above all, discuss your intentions with those closest to you, now.

4. It is a good idea to look over your Living Will once a year, and redate it and initial the new date to make it clear that your wishes are unchanged.

5. Make a copy of the Living Will above for your spouse, if he or she desires. Attach the copy to this page for future reference.

7

Medicare and Social Security

A major expansion of Medicare health benefits was approved by Congress to take effect January 1, 1989. Although there are some new benefits, there are also some new costs.

Under the new Medicare Catastrophic Coverage Act, coverage against catastrophic illness is paid for solely by Medicare beneficiaries. In the past, improvements in Medicare were paid for by workers and their employers. Beginning in 1989, there is an increase in the flat monthly premium that Medicare recipients will have deducted from their monthly Social Security checks. (However, in no case will this reduce Social Security benefits to less than what they are today.) In addition, Medicare-eligible people whose federal income taxes are in excess of $150 pay an additional supplemental premium. This premium is a surcharge to income tax and increases in proportion to tax liability.

NEW BENEFITS

Although the new plan fails to provide insurance protection for the cost of long-term care in a nursing home, it does offer almost total protection for the costs of a hospital stay. The only out-of-pocket cost is a single annual deductible. Part A of Medicare covers the hospital costs, while Part B pays doctors' bills. Prior to the new Medicare act, Medicare Part A provided full coverage for only the first 60 days of a hospital stay. The patient paid a charge of $135 a day for each day hospitalized between 60 and 90 days. For 91 to 150 days, there was a charge of $270 per day. Thereafter, Medicare hospital insurance paid nothing toward hospitalization that was due to a single spell of illness. A person hospitalized because of a second illness would begin the Part A deductible process all over again. Under the new Medicare plan, payment of the annual Medicare Part A deductible entitles the person to up to 365 days of 100 percent coverage while in the hospital. The "spell of illness rule" is no longer in existence, and the patient is no longer required to make any payments in the event he or she is hospitalized for more than 60 days. Also, if a patient pays a deductible during December, there is no additional deductible for a hospitalization beginning in January of the following year. This is done to prevent a patient who has to pay an end-of-year deductible from having to pay the same deductible within a short time period.

Medicare Part A pays 100 percent of the following hospital-related costs:

- operating and recovery room
- semiprivate room and board
- intensive care unit
- drugs furnished by the hospital
- medical supplies
- lab tests, X-rays, and radiation therapy
- appliances
- rehabilitation services
- physical therapy
- cost of special care unit
- stay in a psychiatric hospital, subject to a lifetime limit of 190 days

Medicare Part A does not cover services rendered by doctors while a patient is hospitalized; however, doctors' fees are covered by Medicare Part B.

The new law requires private insurance carriers who provide so-called "medigap" coverage to eliminate from their policies benefits that duplicate those provided by the new act. Your insurer is required to inform you of the changes that it is making by January 31, 1989. The cost savings will be passed through to policyholders in the form of lower premiums; however, this savings may not be much. Since medigap policies pay out most of their benefits to meet the Medicare Part A deductible, they pay out very little in copayments for lengthy hospitalizations that were only partially covered by Medicare under the old law. Because the new law has even higher Part A deductibles, medigap policies will continue to be fairly expensive.

HMOs (Health Maintenance Organizations) or similar medical insurance plans will now have to include the new catastrophic benefits and lower costs in their standard Medicare packages.

One key provision of the new law is the "maintenance of effort" provision. This requires employers who have plans that supplement Medicare to spend at least as much on Medicare-enrolled employees in 1989 and 1990 as they do today. Employers can either pass on the savings under the new law in the form of additional medical coverage, or they can pay employees a direct cash rebate. Companies that currently provide hospitalization coverage that duplicates 50 percent or more of Medicare Part A must pass on their savings in 1989, when Part A's new protection takes effect. In addition, Part B Medicare coverage is also expanded in 1990. If your employer's health plan covers part of your doctors' bills, you may get a second share of savings in 1990. After 1990, employers are no longer required to share insurance savings created by the new law.

Skilled Nursing Care

Under the new plan, Medicare Part A pays for 150 days per year in a skilled nursing facility. In addition, the new law puts a cap on the amount of out-of-pocket cost that a Medicare beneficiary can incur. Also, the new law removes the requirement that you must have been hospitalized within 30 days of admission to a skilled nursing care facility. The new law does not cover custodial care in a nursing home. Any level of care that is less intensive than skilled nursing care is not covered by the new Medicare plan. The nature of the care is what determines whether the cost of a nursing home is covered by Medicare.

Hospice Care

A Medicare beneficiary who is terminally ill may elect to receive hospice care in place of other Medicare benefits under Part A. This type of care, which is oriented toward pain control and supportive services, can be given in the home or in a special facility. Under the new plan, Medicare coverage is unlimited for as long as the physician certifies that hospice care is appropriate.

Home Health Services

Some home health services are covered up to 100 percent by basic Part A Medicare. If set up under a plan of treatment by a doctor and provided at your home or on an outpatient basis, the following services may be covered:

- part-time nursing care
- physical, occupational, or speech therapy
- medical supplies
- part-time services of a home health aide

Medicare Part B

Medicare Part B provides coverage for doctors' bills. You pay a fixed monthly premium of $28.80 per month for Part B coverage. Usually, it is deducted directly from monthly Social Security checks. Under Part B, you pay the first $75 of doctors' bills. Subsequently, Medicare will pay 80 percent of the "reasonable" costs of doctors' fees.

Starting in 1990, the new law puts a cap of $1,370 on your out-of-pocket expenses for Medicare-approved doctor services. Each year this cap will be raised, and Medicare will pay 100 percent of all reasonable expenses above that ceiling.

Prescription Drug Coverage

Previously, Medicare's Part B coverage excluded most of the cost of outpatient prescription drugs. However, under the new law, Medicare pays 50 percent of the cost of all covered outpatient prescription drugs following payment of an annual deductible of $600. This deductible and coinsurance is treated separately from the Part B deductible and coinsurance amounts. This coverage is scheduled to increase to 60 percent in 1992, and to 80 percent thereafter, with the deductible rising to $652. Coverage is limited to prescriptions for a 30-day supply or less and is based on the average wholesale price of the drug.

Other New Benefits

Starting January 1, 1990, Part B of Medicare pays for up to 80 hours a year for in-home care for a chronically dependent individual. This is someone who is dependent on another for help for at least two activities of daily life (eating, dressing, and so on). Respite-care benefits are available for a period of 12 months after meeting either the Part B catastrophic cap or the prescription drug deductible. The care must be given by a Medicare-certified home health agency.

The new law also provides for coverage of the cost of intravenous drug therapy services provided in the home. The coverage includes the cost of nursing, pharmaceuticals and related services, and items needed to administer the drugs. These services are not subject to the Part B Medicare deductible or to coinsurance amounts.

Finally, with respect to intermittent care, beginning in 1990, nursing care and home health-aide services may be provided seven days a week, with one or more visits per day, for up to 38 consecutive days. Eighty percent of the reasonable cost up to the catastrophic limit is covered under Medicare Part B. Thereafter, it pays 100 percent. Medicare will pay the entire reasonable cost from the start if the services are also covered by Part A.

Paying the New Medicare Costs

Cost for the new Medicare plan will be covered in two ways. First, there is the supplemental premium, which is collected with the federal income tax of taxpayers age 65 or over. For 1989, this premium is $22.50 per $150 of tax liability (see figure 25). The maximum premium is $800 per Medicare-eligible individual. If you file a joint return, the supplemental premium rate is the same; however, the premium cap is $1,600 if both filers are each eligible for Medicare for more than six months during the calendar year. If only one person is eligible, the premium tax rate is applied to one-half the joint tax liability. The premium tax rate and the caps are scheduled to increase through 1993. Thereafter, they are indexed annually. (Refer to Figure 27 at the end of the chapter.)

Note that the supplemental premium is not deductible as medical expense.

The second cost is the fixed Part B premium. This premium, which is $28.80 per month in 1989, helps fund the new coverage. This is in addition to any regular annual increase in the Part B premium due to a rise in the overall cost of medical care. The cost of this new catastrophic coverage is scheduled to increase each year through 1993, after which it is indexed to the cost of providing coverage.

Also, beginning in 1991, an additional charge of $1.94 is added to the monthly Part B premium to cover the cost of the new law's prescription drug coverage. This premium also increases through 1993, after which it is indexed.

FIGURE 25   New Medicare Costs

PART A

Year	Supplemental premium	Cap on supplemental premium	Deductible
1988	0	0	$540
1989	$22.50/$150 of Tax Liability	$ 800	$564
1990	$37.50	$ 805	Indexed
1991	$39.00	$ 900	Indexed
1992	$40.50	$ 950	Indexed
1993	$42.00	$1,050	Indexed

PART B

Year	Monthly premium	Deductible	Coinsurance	Out-of-pocket limit
1988	24.80	$75.00	20%	None
1989	28.80	$75.00	20%	$1,370
1990	29.70	$75.00	20%	Indexed
1991	32.20	$75.00	20%	Indexed
1992	34.00	$75.00	20%	Indexed
1993	35.00	$75.00	20%	Indexed

PRESCRIPTION DRUGS

Year	Deductible	Coinsurance
1988	0	0
1989	0	0
1990	$550	20%
1991	$600	50%
1992	$652	40%
1993	N/A	20%

Increases in the Part B premium can cancel out any future cost-of-living increase in Social Security benefits. However, the new law provides that any future Social Security benefit must at least equal what it was in the preceding year. Thus, the increased Medicare Part B premium cost can never exceed the cost-of-living increase for Social Security benefits.

FIGURE 26   Social Security Tax Rates and Maximum Taxable Amounts for the 1980s

Year	Employer and employee tax rate (a)	Self-employed tax rate (a)	Maximum taxable amount
1980	6.13%	8.10%	$25,900
1981	6.65	9.30	29,700
1982	6.70	9.35	32,400
1983	6.70	9.35	35,700
1984	6.70	11.30	37,800
1985	7.05	11.80	39,600
1986	7.15	12.30	42,000
1987	7.15	12.30	43,800
1988	7.51	13.02	45,000
1989	7.51	13.02	(b)
1990	7.65	15.30	(b)

(a) Data for 1986–1990 are from the Social Security Amendments of 1983.

(b) To be determined each year based on increases in average earnings of all employees in the country (whether or not under Social Security).

SOCIAL SECURITY

The Social Security Act of 1935 provides for a broad range of cash and health benefits under (OASDI) Old Age and Survivors Disability Insurance, including old age (retirement), survivors', and disability insurance benefits. These benefits are payable to retired or disabled wage earners and their dependents or, if a wage earner is deceased, to that person's survivors. Taxes paid by employers, employees, and the self-employed are the primary source of both OASDI benefits and hospital insurance benefits (Medicare see figure 26). The Social Security Administration collects these taxes and pays them into the U.S. Treasury, which then allocates them according to a statutory formula to the Federal Old Age and Survivors Insurance Trust Fund, the Federal Disability Insurance Trust Fund, and the Federal Hospital Insurance Trust Fund. (The Social Security Act is found in Title 42 of the United States Code. Title 2 of the Act contains the provisions dealing with OASDI benefits, and the accompanying regulations appear in Title 20 of the Code of Federal Regulations, part 404.)

Social Security Account Number

Every person, whether an employee or self-employed, who is engaged in employment covered by the Social Security Act is required to obtain a Social Security account number from the Social Security Administration. The individual's earnings and Social Security tax payments are credited to this account. This lifetime record becomes the basis for determining the amount of benefits payable to the beneficiary upon eligibility for OASDI or Medicare benefits. The same account number is also used for tax purposes and for certain other federal and state programs.

The person planning for retirement should verify his or her lifetime employment record as indicated in his or her account. The individual should mail a completed copy of Form SSA-7004-PC (see figure 27) to:

Social Security Administration
Wilkes-Barre Data Operations Center
P.O. Box 20
Wilkes-Barre, PA 18703

The form can also be obtained at your local Social Security office.

The time limit for correcting the earnings record is April 15 of the fourth year following the year in which the earnings were made. Under certain circumstances, corrections requested beyond the time limit are permissible.

Establishing Coverage by Social Security

Persons with employee status in covered employment or who are self-employed are eligible for Social Security benefits.

Social Security benefits are based on an individual's fulfillment of the following requirements during his or her working life:

1. The individual must have been an employee or have been self-employed. Workers are considered employees when they are under an employer's control in matters such as being hired or suspended, working set hours, or submitting reports. Corporate officers, full-time salespersons, and homeworkers are ordinarily considered employees. Independent contractors and business partners, on the other hand, are not employees.

2. The individual's job must be covered employment. Workers not considered covered by Social Security include these:

FIGURE 27   Form SSA-7004-PC

SOCIAL SECURITY ADMINISTRATION

Request for Earnings and Benefit Estimate Statement

To receive a free statement of your earnings covered by Social Security and your estimated future benefits, all you need to do is fill out this form. Please print or type your answers. When you have completed the form, fold it and mail it to us.

1. Name shown on your Social Security card:

   First   Middle Initial   Last

2. Your Social Security number as shown on your card:

   ☐☐☐ - ☐☐ - ☐☐☐☐

3. Your date of birth: Month   Day   Year

4. Other Social Security numbers you may have used:

5. Your Sex: ☐ Male   ☐ Female

6. Other names you have used (including a maiden name):

7. Show your actual earnings for last year and your estimated earnings for this year. Include only wages and/or net self-employment income subject to Social Security tax.

   A. Last year's actual earnings:

      $ ☐☐☐,☐☐☐.☐☐
      Dollars only

   B. This year's estimated earnings:

      $ ☐☐☐,☐☐☐.☐☐
      Dollars only

8. Show the age at which you plan to retire:

9. Below, show an amount which you think best represents your future average yearly earnings between now and when you plan to retire. The amount should be a yearly average, not your total future lifetime earnings. Only show earnings subject to Social Security tax.

   Most people should enter the same amount as this year's estimated earnings (the amount shown in 7B). The reason for this is that we will show your retirement benefit estimate in today's dollars, but adjusted to account for average wage growth in the national economy.

   However, if you expect to earn significantly more or less in the future than what you currently earn because of promotions, a job change, part-time work, or an absence from the work force, enter the amount in today's dollars that will most closely reflect your future average yearly earnings. Do not add in cost-of-living, performance, or scheduled pay increases or bonuses.

   Your future average yearly earnings:

   $ ☐☐☐,☐☐☐.☐☐
   Dollars only

10. Address where you want us to send the statement:

    Name

    Street Address (Include Apt. No., P.O. Box, or Rural Route)

    City   State   Zip Code

    I am asking for information about my own Social Security record or the record of a person I am authorized to represent. I understand that if I deliberately request information under false pretenses I may be guilty of a federal crime and could be fined and/or imprisoned. I authorize you to send the statement of my earnings and benefit estimates to me or my representative through a contractor.

    Please sign your name (Do not print)

    Date   (Area Code) Daytime Telephone No.

    ☐ SP

Form SSA-7004-PC-OP2 (6/88) DESTROY PRIOR EDITIONS

Moisten, fold, and seal before mailing.

- federal government employees hired before January 1, 1984
- employees of nonprofit organizations that did not arrange for Social Security coverage prior to January 1, 1984
- state and local government employees for whom coverage has not been arranged
- railroad workers
- some agricultural and domestic workers

3. The individual paid Social Security taxes on wages received or net earnings from self-employment.
4. The individual accumulates sufficient quarters of coverage, based on earned income, to obtain the insured status needed for a particular benefit.

A quarter of coverage (QC) is credited to an individual who is paid wages or earns self-employment income during certain periods. These periods are calendar quarters, which are periods of three calendar months ending March 31, June 30, September 30, or December 31 of any year. The accumulated number of QCs determines insured status, which establishes whether a benefit is payable (see figure 28).

A worker may acquire a QC in several ways:

1. For years prior to 1978, a QC was credited for each time period in which a worker was paid $50 or more in wages in covered employment (except wages for agricultural labor paid after 1954) or for which he or she had been credited with $100 or more of self-employment income.
2. In 1978, an individual was credited with a QC, up to a maximum of four per year, for each $250 of earnings. A higher amount was used in each subsequent year, computed according to a statutory formula based on average annual wages in the nation. The amount required for a QC in 1987 was $470.
3. In any year in which the worker has been credited with the maximum taxable wages for that year, the individual receives credit for four QCs.
4. For pre-1951 wages, QCs are computed according to a special statutory method. A worker not otherwise fully insured is deemed to have one QC for each $400 of total wages from 1937 to 1950 if the individual had at least seven "elapsed years" in the period for determining the worker's fully insured status, and if the worker is fully insured when the QCs determined by this method, added to the QCs credited for periods after 1950, equal the total needed for such status.

FIGURE 28   Work Credit Required for Social Security Retirement Benefits

	You need credit for this much work	
If you reach age 62 in	Years	Quarters
1987–1990	9	36
1991 or after	10	40

There are three types of insured status, depending on the particular benefit: Fully insured, currently insured, and insured for disability benefits. The status determines whether the benefit is payable, not how much is to be paid.

A worker is fully insured for life if the person has forty QCs. A worker with less than forty QCs is deemed fully insured in the following situations:

- The worker died before 1951 with at least six QCs
- The worker has one QC for each calendar year for the period from 1950 or age 21, whichever is later, until retirement age or death

A worker is currently insured when he or she has at least six QCs during the 13-quarter period ending with the quarter in which the person died or became entitled to disability or old-age insurance benefits. A quarter is not counted as part of the 13-quarter period if any part of it was included in a period of disability, except that the first and last quarters of the period of disability may be counted if they are QCs.

A worker has insured status for disability benefits if any of the following apply:

1. The worker would have been fully insured had the worker attained the age of 62 and applied for old-age benefits when disability began
2. In the quarter when the worker's disability begins, the worker

- has at least twenty QCs in the 40-quarter period ending with that quarter
- became disabled in a quarter before the age of 31 and had QCs in one-half of the quarters during the period beginning with the quarter after the quarter in which the person attained the age of 21 and ending with the quarter in which the person became disabled
- is disabled by blindness

Military service before 1957 is generally not covered by Social Security, but wage credits are given for service from September 6, 1940, to December 31, 1956. Persons who served during that period and are still in active service, who died in active service, or who were discharged under conditions other than dishonorable are deemed to have received $160 of covered wages for each month of active service during those particular years. This sum determines the person's insured status to help the person, or his or her dependents or survivors, qualify for Social Security benefits or gain a higher benefit. These wage credits are not given to military personnel who are entitled to a veteran's or federal pension based on those same years of service.

After 1956, military personnel are covered by Social Security on a contributory basis. In addition, for each quarter after 1956 and before 1977, military personnel receive noncontributory wage credits of $300. After 1977, military personnel are deemed to have been paid additional wages of $100 for each $300 of wages received in a calendar year.

Old-Age Benefits: Worker and Spouse

A worker becomes eligible for retirement benefits upon reaching the age of 62, being fully insured, and applying for the benefits. Benefits received between the ages of 62 and 65 are paid at a permanently reduced rate. However, if the worker waits until he or she is 65 to apply for old-age benefits, the benefit is the full primary insurance amount (PIA) to which the person is entitled. At 65, disability benefits automatically become old-age benefits.

The age for full retirement will continue to be 65 through 1999. In 2000, it will begin to rise, reaching 66 in 2005. It will remain at 66 through 2016, and then in 2017 begin another gradual increase until it reaches 67 in 2022.

A person is eligible for Social Security benefits as a spouse (one-half the amount paid to the retired worker), if he or she meets the age or child-care criteria and the definition of a spouse.

The age and child-care standards require that the spouse

- be at least 62, or
- have "in care," at the time of establishing entitlement, a child who is entitled to a child's benefits on the worker's earnings record and who either is under 16 or disabled.

A spouse of the insured is a person who

- has been married to the worker for at least one year
- is the natural parent of the worker's child

- in the month before the spouse married the worker, is entitled to benefits as a spouse, surviving spouse, parent, or disabled child under the Social Security Act or to Railroad Retirement benefits as a surviving spouse, parent, or child (18 or older)

The determination of whether an applicant is a spouse is based on the laws of the state in which the worker has a permanent home when the spouse applies for wife's or husband's benefits. However, even if the applicant would not be considered a spouse under the applicable state law, the Social Security Act still classifies the person as a spouse if the person had a "deemed-valid marriage" with the worker.

A worker's divorced spouse may also receive benefits if the spouse was validly married to the worker for at least ten years immediately before the divorce became final. The divorced spouse must be at least 62, not presently married, and not entitled to an old-age or disability benefit that would be larger than a wife's or husband's full benefit. It is not necessary that the insured worker have attained the age of 62, provided that the divorce has been in effect for at least two years.

A spouse's benefits begin with the first month covered by the application throughout which all other requirements for entitlement are met. The benefits end with the month before the month in which one of the following events first occurs:

1. The spouse becomes entitled to old-age or disability benefits larger than a spouse's full benefit.
2. The spouse is divorced from the worker, unless the spouse meets the requirements for a divorced spouse.
3. A divorced spouse remarries, unless the new spouse is also entitled to Social Security benefits in his or her own right.
4. A child "in care" of a spouse under the age of 62 becomes 16 (unless disabled) and is not otherwise entitled to child's benefits.
5. The worker dies or is no longer entitled to old-age or disability benefits.
6. If the spouse's benefits are based on a deemed-valid marriage, the spouse marries someone other than the insured, or someone also becomes entitled to spouse's benefits based on a deemed-valid marriage.
7. The spouse dies.

Survivor's Benefits

A surviving spouse of a worker who was fully insured when he or she dies is entitled to benefits under the following conditions:

1. The spouse is the insured's widow or widower according to the criteria for a spouse.
2. Any one of the following conditions are met:

   - The spousal relationship to the insured lasted for at least nine months immediately before the worker died.
   - Although the spousal relationship lasted less than nine months, the insured was reasonably expected to live for nine months and died accidentally, died in the line of active military duty, or was previously married to the spouse for at least nine months.
   - The spouse and the worker were natural parents of a child.
   - The spouse was already entitled or could have been entitled to Social Security or Railroad Retirement benefits in the month before the spouse married the insured.

3. The spouse applies for benefits. No application is needed, however, if the spouse was already entitled to wife's or husband's benefits for the month preceding the month in which the worker died and was 65 or not entitled to old-age or disability benefits; or to mother's or father's benefits for the month before the month in which the applicant spouse reached 65.
4. The spouse is at least 60 years old, or is at least 50 years old and disabled.
5. The spouse is not entitled to equal or larger benefits in the spouse's own right.
6. The spouse is unmarried, unless remarriage occurs after the age of 60. However, remarriage of a disabled surviving spouse before the age of 60 does not terminate benefits. For benefits for months beginning with January 1984, remarriage after 50 but before 60 will not disqualify the surviving spouse who is now over age 60, if the individual was entitled to benefits as a disabled surviving spouse at the time of the remarriage or met the disability requirements.

   Survivor's benefits begin with the first month covered by the application in which all requirements for entitlement are met. The entitlement ends at the earliest of the following times:

1. The month before the month of remarriage, unless the spouse is over 60 at the time of remarriage or marries a person already entitled to survivor's, parent's, or disabled child's benefits.
2. The month before the month when the spouse becomes entitled to equal or larger old-age benefits.
3. The second month after the month of recovery if the survivor's benefit is based on a disability, unless the person is already participating in an approved program of vocational rehabilitation at the time the impairment is no longer disabling, and SSA approves continuation in the program.
4. The month before the month in which another person becomes entitled to spouse's or survivor's benefits if the survivor's benefit is based on a deemed-valid marriage.

A surviving spouse of a deceased, fully or currently insured worker may qualify for mother's or father's benefits, which are different from widow or widower's benefits, under the following conditions:

1. The person is the widow or widower of the insured.
2. The person applies for benefits or was entitled to spouse's benefits for the month before the insured died.
3. The person is unmarried.
4. The person is not entitled to widow or widower's benefits (for example, because the person is younger than 60) or to an old-age benefit equal to or larger than the full mother's or father's benefit.
5. The person has "in care" the insured's child who is entitled to child's benefits and is under 16 or disabled.

A surviving divorced spouse may be entitled to mother's or father's benefits under the same general conditions. However, it must be established that the divorced spouse is the parent of the child or that the divorced spouse was married to the worker when either party adopted the other's child or when both adopt a child who was then under 18.

A child of a deceased worker is entitled to child's benefits if the child meets the relationship, dependency, and age requirements.

A parent of a deceased worker who was fully insured is entitled to benefits if all the following conditions are met:

1. The parent is considered a "parent" under the law—that is, the applicant was the mother or father of the insured, the adoptive parent who adopted the insured before he or she reached the age of 16, or the stepparent of the insured through a marriage contracted before the insured became 16. The laws of the state in which the insured

    had a permanent home at death govern determinations of parentage and the validity of the parent's marriage.

2. The parent is 62 or older.
3. The parent has not married since the insured died.
4. The parent applies for benefits.
5. The parent is not entitled to an old-age benefit at least as large as the worker's benefit.
6. The parent was dependent on the insured at the time of the latter's death, i.e., he or she was receiving one-half support from the insured at the time of death or, if the insured was disabled, at the time of the onset of disability. Proof of such support must be filed within two years after disability began or after death, depending on which date is the basis of the claim for support. Failure to file such evidence may be excused in certain extenuating circumstances.

Parent's benefits begin with the first month covered by the application in which all requirements for entitlement are met. Entitlement ends with the month before the month in which the parent dies, becomes entitled to an equal or larger old-age benefit, or marries a person not already entitled to Social Security benefits.

Older persons, who had little or no chance to become fully insured during their working years and several years ago became 72 years old, may qualify for a special payment. A person is entitled to this payment under the following conditions:

1. The person became 72 before 1968, or had at least three QCs between 1966 and the year the age of 72 was reached.
2. The person resides in one of the 50 states, the District of Columbia, or the Northern Mariana Islands.
3. The person applies.
4. The person is an American citizen, a citizen of the Northern Mariana Islands, or a permanent resident alien with at least five years of continuous residence.

Entitlement to the special payment begins with the first month covered by the application in which all requirements for entitlement are met and ends with the month before the month of the person's death.

Increases in Benefits

Cost-of-living increases in benefits are payable in January of each year for the previous December's benefits. The increase occurs in years when increases in the Consumer Price Index (CPI) or the average annual wages in the base quarter exceeds zero percent, and when the lower of these figures is less than 20 percent of the combined Social Security Trust Fund ratios. The lower rate (CPI or average wages increase), known as the applicable increase percentage, is multiplied by the worker's PIA (Primary Insurance Amount). The PIA is the basis for calculating the increased benefit.

Workers who delay retirement beyond the age of 65 and consequently do not receive benefits are entitled to an increase in old-age benefits of 1/4 of a percent for each month they postpone benefits, the equivalent to 3 percent per year. This rate will increase to 3.5 percent per year for workers reaching 65 in 1990. It will continue to increase by 1/2 of a percent per year in subsequent even-numbered years until the year 2008, when the credit will reach eight percent per year. This credit is applied only to retirement delayed until the age of 70.

Decreases in Benefits

Variously known as reductions, deductions, nonpayments, and suspensions, decreases in benefits are required in certain situations.

Family Maximum. The Social Security Act limits the amount of monthly benefits that can be paid for any month, based on the earnings record of a particular worker. If the total benefits to which all persons are entitled on the one worker's earnings record exceed the maximum amount prescribed by law, those benefits must be reduced so that they do not exceed the maximum.

The formula for calculating the family maximum for a worker retiring, becoming 62, or dying in 1988 is as follows:

150 percent of the first $407 of PIA, plus 272 percent of the excess PIA over $407 to $767, plus 134 percent of the excess PIA over $571 to $745, plus 175 percent of the excess PIA over $767.

The dollar amounts in the formula, known as bend points, are increased annually according to the cost-of-living formula.

Example: Al retired in 1987 with a PIA of $774. He has a wife and two dependent children. His family maximum will be

150 percent of $407	=	$ 611.00
272 percent of $181	=	$ 492.00
134 percent of $179	=	$ 240.00
175 percent of $ 7	=	$ 12.00
Total	=	$1,355

Thus, Al's maximum family benefit will be $1,355.

Where the total of the benefits for which each individual family member qualifies exceeds the family maximum amount, each benefit, except the worker's, is reduced proportionately.

Example: Al's PIA is $774. His wife, 62, is entitled to a wife's benefit of $387, and each of his two children is also entitled to $387. The total of the four benefits is $1,935, which exceeds the family maximum of $1,355, for a difference of $580. Since the wife and children are entitled to the same amount of benefit, each of their benefits will be reduced by the same amount. The excess of $580 divided by 3 = $193. Therefore, Al will receive $774, his wife $194, and each of the children $194.

The family maximum is not applied until other deductions have been made, such as for excess earnings after retirement, failure to have a child in care, penalties for failure to report certain events to the Social Security Administration, and refusal to accept rehabilitation services.

Example: Al's wife was employed full time during 1988 and earned $9,000. Her earnings exceed the exempt amount of $6,120 for that year, and, therefore, her benefits are reduced by $1 for every $2 of excess earnings ($2,880). Her benefit entitlement is reduced by $1440 from $4,644 annually ($387 per month) to $3,204 annually ($267 per month).

This reduction for excess earnings is taken before the reductions for exceeding the family maximum occurs. The total entitlements of each family member are:

$$\$774 + \$267 + \$387 + \$387 = \$1,815.$$

This sum still exceeds the family maximum of $1,355 by $460. Each dependent's benefit is reduced proportionately by $153 to $114, $234, and $234, respectively.

Where the worker first became entitled to disability benefits on or after July 1, 1980, the family benefits are subject to a further possible reduction. The total family benefits of a disbled worker is the smaller of (1) 85 percent of the worker's average monthly earnings (or 100 percent of the worker's PIA, if larger), or (2) 150 percent of the worker's PIA.

Example: Oscar became disabled in August 1988. His average indexed monthly earnings (AIME) was $600, and his PIA was $371. The maximum family benefit is the smaller of:

1. the larger of 85 percent of AIME ($510) or 100 percent of the PIA ($371), or
2. 150 percent of the PIA ($557)

Therefore, the family maximum is $510. Benefits for a divorced spouse or a surviving divorced spouse are not reduced by the family maximum rule.

Early Retirement.   The basic benefits of a worker and his or her dependents and survivors are reduced by early retirement. The wage earner's benefits are reduced $5/9$ of 1 percent for each month from the month the worker becomes 62 or in which the worker becomes entitled to old-age benefits, and the month before the month in which the worker turns 65. For example, if a worker whose PIA is $450 decides to retire on his or her 62nd birthday, which is 35 months from the month preceding his or her 65th birthday, the reduction would be calculated as follows:

$$\$450 \times {}^{5}/_{9} \times {}^{1}/_{100} \times 35 = \$87.50$$

Thus, the reduced monthly benefit is $362.50 ($450 − $87.50). Slightly different formulas are used for the reductions in dependents' and survivors' benefits where the beneficiary becomes entitled before attaining the age of 65.

The age for full retirement will continue at 65 through 1999, then rise gradually each year until reaching 66 in 2005. There will be another gradual increase in 2017 until it reaches 67 by 2022. Workers and their spouses reaching the age of 62 after 1999 and electing early retirement will have their benefits reduced by $5/9$ of 1 percent formula for the first 36 months of reduction and $5/12$ of 1 percent in any subsequent months.

Excess Earnings.   Deductions are made from the monthly benefits payable to a worker who is under 70 and to his or her dependents for each month in which the worker is charged with earnings in excess of certain amounts. A similar deduction is made in the dependent's benefits when the dependent has excess earnings. These rules do not apply to Social Security benefits based on disability, to persons who are 70 or older, or to work performed outside the United States not covered by Social Security. Likewise, a divorced spouse's benefits are not reduced because of the insured's excess earnings, provided the divorce has been in effect for at least two years.

The maximum amount that a beneficiary (worker, spouse, parent) betweeen 65 and 70 might earn in 1988 without affecting his or her own benefits or those of dependents is $8,400 ($700 per month). A beneficiary under 65 might earn in 1988 up to $6,120 ($510 per month in the year of initial entitlement). Periodic increases in these ceilings are provided for by law as a function of the cost-of-living escalator provision.

Until 1990, the amount of the deduction in benefits is one dollar for every two dollars earned over the annual exempt amount. In 1990, only one dollar in every three dollars will be deducted from the benefit.

However, an individual is entitled to one grace year, usually the calendar year during which retirement occurs, when excess earnings are not offset against old-age benefits. This situation occurs when a retiree or a survivor, entitled to benefits, does not receive excess earnings for at least one month, called a nonservice month.

Other grace years occur when there is a break of at least one month between entitlement to different types of benefits. The new grace year begins in the first taxable year after the break in which a nonservice month occurs. Similarly, a person entitled to child's, mother's, or father's benefits is also entitled to a termination grace year in the year in which the beneficiary's entitlement to benefits ceases, unless death is the reason for termination or the beneficiary is entitled to another Social Security benefit in the month following termination. No nonservice month is required for a termination grace year.

Earnings include wages for services in a taxable year, as well as net earnings minus net losses from self-employment in a taxable year. *Wages* in this context refers to gross income of an employee, and includes all cash pay for domestic service in a private home, service not in the course of the employer's trade or business, and agricultural labor. All remuneration, cash or noncash, is counted for work as a homeworker. Pay for active military or naval service in the American armed forces performed in the United States is also included.

Earnings do not include interest, dividends, annuities, pensions, or royalties attributable to a copyright or patent obtained prior to the taxable year in which the individual attained the age of 65, if the copyright or patent is on property created by that individual's own personal efforts. Also excluded from gross earnings is self-employment income received in a year after the initial year of entitlement that is not attributable to services performed after the first month the individual became entitled to benefits. However, these become "significant services" if they include significant work activity performed by the individual in the operation or management of a trade, profession, or business, which can be related to the income received. Once determined to be based on significant services performed after retirement, income will be counted as self-employment income under the earnings test. Services for several trades or businesses may accumulate into significant services. The individual claiming not to have countable royalties or self-employment income has the burden of proving that such increases may be excluded.

Ordinarily, an application for benefits should be filed at the time the applicant satisfies the conditions of entitlement. Filing before the first month of entitlement is deemed to have been filed in the first month, if the conditions of entitlement have been satisfied before the SSA makes a final decision on the claim.

Filing at a time after the applicant became entitled, or even ceased to be entitled to benefits, is acceptable. Applications for disability benefits are ordinarily accepted up to 12 months after disability has ended, and if the delay is due to the applicant's physical or mental condition, up to 36 months later, if the person is still alive. Applications for old-age and survivor's benefits that are filed later than the first month after entitlement result in payments of benefits for only up to six months immediately preceding the filing. An application for a lump-sum death payment must be filed within two years after the death of the insured, unless an extension is granted for good cause or because the deceased was in the armed services and died overseas.

Generally, an applicant must submit evidence to prove his or her identity and fulfillment of all the requirements for the benefit being sought.

Original records are preferred, but properly certified copies are accepted. Birth certificates, religious birth records, marriage licenses and/or certificates, decrees of divorce, and death certificates are the usual documents needed for most benefits.

Taxation of Benefits

A portion of all OASDI benefits may be subject to federal income taxation. The benefits will be included in the gross income of the person who has the legal right to receive the benefits. The amount includable in a taxable year will be the lesser of

1. one-half of the amount of Social Security benefits (SSB) received, or
2. one-half of the difference between the sum of taxpayer's modified adjusted gross income (MGI) plus one-half of the amount of Social Security benefits (SSB) received, minus the base amount (BA). Expressed as a formula, this alternative reads

$$\tfrac{1}{2}\,[(MGI + \tfrac{1}{2}\,SSB) - BA] = \text{amount includable in gross income}$$

The terms are defined as follows:

1. The "amount of Social Security benefits received" means the benefit payments after statutory reductions and adjustments have been made. Amounts withheld to pay Medicare Part B premiums will count as benefits received. Repayments of benefits should also be deducted from the amount of benefits received in the taxable year in which the repayment is made.
2. "Modified adjusted gross income" is the taxpayer's adjusted gross income plus any deduction taken for foreign earned income, exclusions for certain U.S.-possessions-source income, and tax-exempt interest.
3. The base amount is:

   - $32,000 for a married individual filing a joint return with his or her spouse
   - $25,000 for single individuals and married persons who live apart from their spouses for the entire year and who file a separate return
   - nothing for a married individual who does not live apart from the spouse for the entire year and who does not file a joint return

   Example 1: Sam, retired and a widower, receives $8,000 annually in Social Security benefits, $20,000 in a pension, $4,000 in dividends and $9,000 in tax-exempt interest. The amount includable in his gross income is the lesser of $4,000 (one-half his Social Security benefits) or

$$1/2 \ [\$33,000 + 1/2 \ (8,000) - 25,000] =$$
$$1/2 \ [\$33,000 + 4,000 - 25,000] =$$
$$1/2 \ [\$12,000] = \$6,000$$

Sam, therefore, has taxable Social Security benefits of $4,000 (the lesser amount).

   Example 2: John and Mary, 72 and 71, receive a total of $12,000 in Social Security benefits, $1,000 in dividends, and $5,000 in tax-exempt interest. John is also self-employed and earns $20,000, while Mary earns $15,000. They file a joint income tax return. The amount includable in their gross income is the lesser of $6,000 (one-half their Social Security benefits) or

$$1/2 \ [\$35,000 + 1,000 + 5,000 \ 1/2 \ (12,000) - 32,000] =$$
$$1/2 \ [\$41,000 + 6,000 - 32,000] =$$
$$1/2 \ [\$15,000] = \$7,500$$

John and Mary, therefore, have taxable Social Security benefits of $6,000.

Estimating Your Retirement Benefit Amount

The question most people want answered about Social Security benefits is, "How much will my monthly check be?" The answer: It depends on your annual earnings during your working years, your year of birth, and your retirement age.

Figuring the benefit amount is complex. What's more, to compute the exact amount, you need government figures that are released on a year-to-year basis. As a result, you cannot figure an exact amount in advance of the year you become eligible to collect benefits. You can only get a rough idea of how much your benefits will be in 1989 dollars. Your actual benefit check will reflect cost-of-living increases between now and when you start collecting.

With this in mind, estimate your monthly benefits by following these eight steps:

1. Calculate past earnings. You need to know the amount of your earnings that were subject to Social Security tax every year since 1951, or, if later, the year you reached 22. You can have the Social Security Administration send you this information by filing Form SSA-7004 PC (see figure 27). You can obtain the form from your local Social Security office.

2. Estimate future earnings. Assume your annual income that is subject to Social Security tax remains the same between now and retirement.

3. Adjust for inflation. Social Security benefits depend upon your annual earnings during your working years. But because of inflation and cost-of-living wage adjustments, your earnings from prior years tend to be much lower than your present earnings. The Social Security rules take this into account by translating your prior earnings into current dollars. This is done by multiplying each year's earnings by the appropriate factors based on your index year. The index year used to translate your Social Security earnings into present dollars is the second year before the year you become eligible for Social Security benefits (that is, when you reach the age of 62 or become disabled).

    Example: Mrs. Grant was born in 1929, so she becomes 62 in 1991. That also means her index year for retirement benefits is 1989—regardless of when she actually retires.

4. Multiply actual earnings by the factors in the appropriate index year. Figure 29 gives the calculations for boosting Mrs. Grant's earnings to reflect their equivalent in 1986 dollars, since 1986 is the latest year for which indexes are available. When Mrs. Grant's actual benefits are determined, they will be in 1989 dollars. Note: We are assuming that Mrs. Grant stops working just before the year she becomes 62. If she worked longer, the extra year of earnings would be included on the chart. And in step 6, they could be used to replace lower earning years for calculating the size of the benefit entitlement. Bear in mind also that when an individual does work beyond the age of 62, the later earnings are not indexed.

5. Determine the number of years to be used in calculating your benefits. This is determined by counting the number of years between (1) the later of your reaching the age of 22 or 1951 and (2) the year preceding your 62nd birthday, and then subtracting five from the result (see figure 30). For Mrs. Grant, this is thirty-five (as it is for all born after 1928). However, in figuring benefits for individuals who are disabled before reaching the age of 47, fewer than five years are subtracted: If under the age of 27, don't deduct any years; deduct one year if 27 to 31 years old, two years if 32 to 36 years old, three years if 37 to 41 years old, and four years if 42 to 46 years old.

6. Determine which years are your "benefit computation years." These are the number of years in step 5 with the highest indexed earnings (column F). That means Mrs. Grant can disregard her earnings in 1951–1955.

7. Determine your average indexed monthly earnings (AIME): Total the indexed earnings for your computation years and divide by the number of months in those years. Mrs. Grant takes her $970,640 total earnings for the computation years (1956–1990) and divides it by 420 months (35 years times 12 months per year). Her AIME is $2,311.05, which is rounded down to $2,311. This is the foundation of any benefits she will receive from Social Security.

8. Calculate your Primary Insurance Amount (PIA). Your PIA is the basic monthly Social Security retirement benefit. The system is skewed to provide proportionately more benefits for the bottom dollars you earn and proportionately fewer benefits for your top dollars of earnings.
    —Multiply the first $319 of AIME by 90 percent: $287.
    —Multiple the next $1,922 by 32 percent: $615
    —Multiply any excess by 15 percent: $10.
    Thus, Mrs. Grant's PIA would be $912 (retrement at the age of 65).

FIGURE 29   Calculation Table for Figuring Your Indexed Earnings

A Calendar Year	B Social Security Wage Base	C Enter Your Taxable Earnings	×	D Index Factor	=	E Indexed Earnings	F High Years
1951	$ 3,600	_____		6.2		_____	____
1952	3,600	_____		5.8		_____	____
1953	3,600	_____		5.5		_____	____
1954	3,600	_____		5.5		_____	____
1955	4,200	_____		5.2		_____	____
1956	4,200	_____		4.9		_____	____
1957	4,200	_____		4.8		_____	____
1958	4,200	_____		4.7		_____	____
1959	4,800	_____		4.5		_____	____
1960	4,800	_____		4.3		_____	____
1961	4,800	_____		4.2		_____	____
1962	4,800	_____		4.0		_____	____
1963	4,800	_____		3.9		_____	____
1964	4,800	_____		3.8		_____	____
1965	4,800	_____		3.7		_____	____
1966	6,600	_____		3.5		_____	____
1967	6,600	_____		3.3		_____	____
1968	7,800	_____		3.1		_____	____
1969	7,800	_____		2.9		_____	____
1970	7,800	_____		2.8		_____	____
1971	7,800	_____		2.7		_____	____
1972	9,000	_____		2.4		_____	____
1973	10,800	_____		2.3		_____	____
1974	13,200	_____		2.2		_____	____
1975	14,100	_____		2.0		_____	____
1976	15,300	_____		1.9		_____	____
1977	16,500	_____		1.8		_____	____
1978	17,700	_____		1.6		_____	____
1979	22,900	_____		1.5		_____	____
1980	25,900	_____		1.4		_____	____
1981	29,700	_____		1.3		_____	____
1982	32,400	_____		1.2		_____	____
1983	35,700	_____		1.1		_____	____
1984	37,800	_____		1.0		_____	____
1985	39,600	_____		1.0		_____	____
1986	42,000	_____		1.0		_____	____
1987	43,800	_____		1.0		_____	____
1988	45,000	_____		1.0		_____	____

FIGURE 29   Calculation Table for Figuring Your Indexed Earnings (continued)

		Example			
A Year	B Social Security Wage Base	C Mrs. Grant's SS Earnings	D Index Factor	E Mrs. Grant's Indexed Earnings	F High Years
1951	$ 3,600	$ 0	6.2	$ 0	$ 0
1952	3,600	2,200	5.8	12,760	0
1953	3,600	2,500	5.5	13,750	0
1954	3,600	2,600	5.5	14,300	0
1955	4,200	2,800	5.2	14,560	0
1956	4,200	3,100	4.9	15,190	15,190
1957	4,200	3,300	4.8	15,840	15,840
1958	4,200	3,700	4.7	17,390	17,390
1959	4,800	3,800	4.5	17,100	17,100
1960	4,800	4,000	4.3	17,200	17,200
1961	4,800	4,100	4.2	17,220	17,220
1962	4,800	4,300	4.0	17,200	17,200
1963	4,800	4,600	3.9	17,940	17,940
1964	4,800	4,800	3.8	18,240	18,240
1965	4,800	4,800	3.7	17,760	17,760
1966	6,600	5,800	3.5	20,300	20,300
1967	6,600	6,100	3.3	20,130	20,130
1968	7,800	6,500	3.1	20,150	20,150
1969	7,800	7,000	2.9	20,300	20,300
1970	7,800	7,600	2.8	21,280	21,280
1971	7,800	7,800	2.7	21,060	21,060
1972	9,000	9,000	2.4	21,600	21,600
1973	10,800	10,800	2.3	24,840	21,840
1974	13,200	13,200	2.2	29,040	29,040
1975	14,100	14,100	2.0	28,200	28,200
1976	15,300	15,300	1.9	29,070	29,070
1977	16,500	16,500	1.8	29,700	29,700
1978	17,700	17,700	1.6	28,320	28,320
1979	22,900	22,900	1.5	34,350	34,350
1980	25,900	25,900	1.4	36,260	36,260
1981	29,700	29,700	1.3	38,610	38,610
1982	32,400	32,400	1.2	38,880	38,880
1983	35,700	35,700	1.1	39,270	39,270
1984	37,800	37,800	1.0	37,800	37,800
1985	39,600	39,600	1.0	39,600	39,600
1986	42,000	42,000	1.0	42,000	42,000
1987	43,800	43,800	1.0	43,800	43,800
1988	45,000	45,000	1.0	45,000	45,000
1989		45,000	1.0	45,000	45,000
1990		45,000	1.0	45,000	45,000

FIGURE 30   Years of Earnings Used to Compute Your Retirement Benefit Under Social Security

Year you were born	Year you reach 62	Years needed
1917	1979	23
1918	1980	24
1919	1981	25
1920	1982	26
1921	1983	27
1922	1984	28
1923	1985	29
1924	1986	30
1925	1987	31
1926	1988	32
1927	1989	33
1928	1990	34
1929 or later	1991 or later	35*

*Maximum number of years that count

Note: The "bend points" (that is, $319 and $1,922) at which the percentages change are linked to inflation. However, the bend points for the year you reach the age of 62 are the ones you use to figure benefits, regardless of when you actually start collecting them.

Cost-of-Living Increases

You are eligible for cost-of-living increases starting with the year you reach the age of 62. (The government adds these in automatically when calculating your benefit checks.) Therefore, the PIA represents benefits expressed in dollars of the year you reach 62. If you wait until 65 to start collecting, the actual amount you receive would be somewhat larger, the exact amount depending on the cost-of-living hikes during the next three years.

However, to receive 100 percent of the inflation–adjusted PIA, you must retire at the age of 65. The PIA is the monthly benefit you receive if you start collecting benefits at 65. If you elect to start getting benefits sooner, the size of your monthly checks is reduced to reflect the fact that you'll be getting a larger number of checks over your lifetime.

Early Retirement Benefits

Early retirees receive lower monthly benefits. If you retire between the ages of 62 and 65 your full benefit is reduced by $5/9$ of 1 percent for each month you receive your benefits before reaching the age of 65. So, if you retire at 62, you get 80 percent of your PIA each month. If you retire at the age of 62½, you get 90 percent of your PIA. In Mrs. Grant's case, her PIA at the age of 62 would be 80 percent of $912, or $730.

On the other hand, you receive benefits for a longer time if you retire at 62 instead of at 65. So by retiring early, you may get more dollars back from Social Security during your lifetime than if you retired later. To reach the break-even point, you must receive benefits for about 15 years beyond retiring at 65 to recover the three years of benefits you would have received if you had retired at 62. However, remember that when the normal retirement age is raised from 65 to 67, early retirement benefits will gradually be reduced from 80 percent to 70 percent of the amount available at normal retirement age for taxpayers born after 1937.

Early benefits are also reduced for spouses and widows and widowers. A spouse's insurance benefits are reduced by 0.69444 percent of your PIA for each month of entitlement before the age of 65. For example, at 65, your spouse is entitled to 50 percent of your PIA. If she were 62, she would get only 37.5 percent (75 percent of the 50 percent figure). Benefits for widows and widowers are reduced by 0.475 percent of your PIA for each month of entitlement between the ages of 60 and 65. Your surviving spouse at 60 would therefore get 71.5 percent of your PIA. There is no additional reduction when benefits for widows and widowers are payable before the age of 60 on account of disability.

Suppose you retire at 62 and start collecting reduced retirement benefits. But then you return to work a year later. Result: Your benefits may be increased when you reach 65.

Bigger Benefits for Working Past The Age of 65

Suppose you work for some time past the age of 65 and earn enough that you cannot collect any retirement benefits during your working years. In that event, you will be entitled to even bigger benefit checks once you do start receiving them (see figure 31). (At 70, you can start collecting Social Security retirement benefits regardless of how much you earn.) The additional money is based on what is known as the "delayed retirement credit." The size of it depends on when you become 65 and how long you delay receiving benefits.

FIGURE 31   Delayed Retirement Credit

Year you Attain Age 65	Monthly Percentage	Yearly Percentage
Prior to 1982	$1/12$ of 1%	1%
1982 – 1989	$1/4$ of 1%	3%
1990 – 1991	$7/24$ of 1%	3.5%
1992 – 1993	$1/3$ of 1%	4%
1994 – 1995	$3/8$ of 1%	4.5%
1996 – 1997	$5/12$ of 1%	5%
1998 – 1999	$11/24$ of 1%	5.5%
2000 – 2001	$1/2$ of 1%	6%
2002 – 2003	$13/24$ of 1%	6.5%
2004 – 2005	$7/12$ of 1%	7%
2006 – 2007	$5/8$ of 1%	7.5%
2008 or later	$2/3$ of 1%	8%

For example, based on a PIA of $912, someone who reaches the age of 65 in 1994 and delays receiving benefits for one year would increase his or her monthly benefit checks by $41 ($912 × .045).

8

Investing Basics

Although preretirement and postretirement investment portfolios should each have both income and accumulation aspects, the preretirement portfolio should be more heavily skewed toward accumulation for later use. The postretirement portfolio should show a greater allocation of investment resources toward income-producing vehicles, with a portion allocated for accumulation in order to be able to create a greater income in the future as inflation erodes some of the purchasing power of current income-producing investments.

You can use different investment management techniques as you create your own portfolios and consider the different investment alternatives available to you.

DETERMINING YOUR RISK AND RETURN PREFERENCES

The individual investor has the widest possible range of investor characteristics, needs, desires, and abilities. However, one universal trait is risk aversion. All rational investors, regardless of circumstance, are risk-averse. That is, in risk and return terms, an investor will be willing to take additional investment risk only if there is the likelihood of obtaining additional return relative to his or her current situation.

Investment objectives can be expressed in terms of return and risk; the higher the potential return, the higher the potential risk. In addition, risk and return preferences can often be considered in terms of life cycle stages. That is, one's level of risk acceptance or aversion can be determined by the current stage of his or her lifetime or career.

In the early career stage, assets are small relative to liabilities, especially when liabilities include a large house mortgage and debts from credit purchases. Priorities typically include savings for liquidity purposes, life insurance for death protection, and finally, investments. However, because individuals in this stage have a very long time for accumulation, with a potential growing flow of income, higher risk tends to be undertaken in the hopes of higher gains. It is hoped that possible losses can be made up because of the amount of time remaining to accumulate dollars for future use.

With the mid-career individual, assets equal or exceed liabilities, savings and life insurance programs are typically under way, and a basic investment program has begun. At this time, while the time for accumulation is still relatively strong, capital preservation tends to become more and more important. Individuals in this stage tend to undertake some high risk, while at the same time begin to allocate a greater number of resources toward conservative investments for accumulation.

In the late-career or brink-of-retirement situation, the individual's time for accumulation has diminished, and the reality of the need for income in the near future from investments draws nearer. At this point in time, assets tend to exceed liabilities; savings, pension plans, and life insurance programs are near completion; and for many the house mortgage has been paid off. Income tends to be made up mainly of Social Security benefits, other pension payments, and investment returns. The investment portfolio is typically shifted to significantly lower-return, lower-risk assets. Inflation and other economic worries tend to become major considerations, and individuals recognize the need to have some additional accumulation of assets in order to make up any income shortfall at some time in the future.

Exactly where each investor fixes his or her risk return trade-off at various life cycle stages depends on individual circumstances and individual risk-taking attitudes. In effect, an individual's risk tolerance is unique and subject to changes influenced by the investor's wealth position, health, family situation, age, and temperament. Any investor must be alert to changes in objectives and be prepared to rebalance his or her portfolio accordingly. Figure 33 lists investments according to generally conceded levels of risk. A careful study of this listing should enable you to position yourself and your investments accordingly.

At whatever stage in the life cycle you are, or whatever your risk return preference is, remember that investment management is a process— an integrated set of activities that, when combined in a logical, orderly manner, produces a desired result. Thus, in the ongoing portfolio management process, one must do the following:

- Set objectives, constraints, and preferences.
- Develop strategies and implement those through the choice of various investments.
- Monitor market conditions and your circumstances.
- Make portfolio adjustments as appropriate to reflect any significant changes in any of the variables mentioned above.

When monitoring your portfolio, remember that it is not how well your portfolio does versus other investments that is important but, rather, how well your portfolio meets the needs of your particular situation and helps you achieve your specific objectives.

CREATING YOUR INVESTMENT PORTFOLIO

Each person is an individual with his or her own unique needs. Because of this, there is an endless variety of investment mixes that can be used in creating the desired portfolio to help you meet your needs and objectives. However, there are a few general characteristics that apply to most people.

At younger ages, there is more time left for money to work for you. Because of this, people at younger ages are in an accumulation mode and, thus, have this as a more general objective for their investment portfolio. Younger employees will receive annual salary increases to help counter inflation and can allocate a portion of these increases for future growth in their investment portfolios.

Middle-aged individuals and independent businesspersons or professionals increase their income by raising prices or fees. At this age, there is still an accumulation phase; however, the phase becomes a more conservative one, in which growth is the primary objective, but less risk is tolerated.

Finally, as one gets close to retirement, one must be concerned with having money work to its maximum capacity in order to replace lost income from work after retirement. For most of us, after retirement we can no longer count on salary increases or raising our prices or fees, or on

FIGURE 32   Investments Classified by Level of Risk

1. Very High-Risk Investments—a sophisticated form of gambling

Commodities futures
Options: puts and calls
Collectibles
Oil and gas drilling ventures
Raw land
Gold, silver, and other precious metals
Penny stocks
Foreign stocks
Margin accounts

2. High-Risk Investments—containing elements of speculation

Common stocks of low quality
New issues of stocks and bonds
Speculative grade bonds with the following ratings:
    Standard & Poor BB, B, CCC, CC, D
    Moody Ba, B, Caa, Ca, C

3. Moderate-Risk Investments—offering regular income and potential long-term growth

"Blue chip" common stocks and preferred stocks
Investment-grade corporate and municipal bonds with the following ratings:
    Standard & Poor AAA, AA, A, BBB
    Moody Aaa, Aa, A, Baa
Variable annuities
Investment real estate other than your home
Stock and bond mutual funds whose goals are income and long-term growth

4. Minimum-Risk Investments—offering safety, liquidity, and good yield

Bank money market deposit accounts
Money-market mutual funds
Insured certificates of deposit
U.S. Treasury paper: bills and notes
Tax-exempt bond mutual funds
Individual tax-exempt municipal bonds rated AAA
U.S. government savings bonds
Federal agency bonds: GNMA, FNMA
(Other minimum-risk investments include the equity in your home, fixed annuities, and cash value life insurance.)

other pay increases we have become accustomed to in the past. We must be sure that we have accumulated enough in income-producing assets to help take us through our retirement years in a comfortable manner.

Following are a few strategies you may wish to adopt in creating your own personal investment portfolio.

Diversification

Diversification, or spreading your investible assets among a group of different investments, is really insurance against a severe crisis every few years and avoidance of the old "feast or famine" characteristic of the investment markets. Diversification is used to create a margin of safety in the portfolio by spreading your investible assets among various industries, companies, and geographic areas.

There are various degrees of risk everywhere in life. All investments have an element of risk no matter how well we research and watch them. Thus, it is necessary for us to take any available precaution to prevent a catastrophe in case the unforeseen or unexpected takes place.

There is a general rule that you should not invest more than five percent of your investible assets in any one stock or more than 15 percent in any one industry. However, this principle is a guide and not a fixed rule to which we must strictly adhere.

Diversification is used to reduce risk and help ensure a consistent return for the investor.

The Total-Return Approach

The principle of total return is a consideration of dividend yield plus capital gain plus interest. Many investors, especially those already retired, get trapped by positioning all their funds in fixed-income instruments to generate a current safe income, without considering the overall return of the entire portfolio.

Even someone who is retired needs to have continued growth to provide increased income in future years. The total return approach will allow you the increased growth you may need, while at the same time providing a generous income prior to entering your retirement years.

Dollar Cost-Averaging

Dollar cost-averaging is an old idea that requires, at times, an extreme amount of patience. It is one of the most widely endorsed strategies for long-term growth in stocks, mutual funds, or just about any other liquid asset that fluctuates in value. It can work well for small or large investors and is a good tool for people who are unable or unwilling to devote a lot of time to following the daily ups and downs of the various investment markets.

Dollar cost-averaging calls for investors to make purchases of the same security in equal dollar amounts at regular intervals over an extended period of time. This insures that you will not put all your money into the investment at a single inopportune moment. It allows simple mathematics to work in your favor. Regular investments of the same amount of money will buy more shares of stock or mutual fund when its price is depressed and fewer shares when the price is high.

Let's take an example. Suppose you put $1,000 into a mutual fund every April 1st regardless of the market conditions. The first year, with the fund's net asset value at $10, you buy 100 shares. The next year, with the net asset value at $12.50, you buy 80 shares. The third year, with the net asset value at $8, you buy 125 shares. Shortly thereafter, the net asset value rises again to $10. At that point, the fund stands exactly where it was when you bought it. Aside from any dividends or other distributions, you might expect that your investment was just at the break-even point; however, you would actually show a $50.00 profit, since the $3,000 you have put into the fund has bought you 305 shares worth $3,050.

This effect increases with the amount of money involved, the volatility of the investment, and the amount of time you follow such a strategy. However, you must remember that dollar cost-averaging assumes that the investment you choose will not decline in value and never recover. You must be confident in this assumption if you are using dollar cost-averaging, since you are making a long-term commitment and a considerable amount of money to this type of investment strategy.

There will always be times during dollar cost-averaging when you wonder whether you are simply not throwing good money after bad. Yet this system is a good way to impose discipline on yourself and to minimize the effects of the emotions that can affect anyone's financial planning.

Fear and greed often persuade people to buy when prices are high and to sell when prices are low, which is just the opposite of what you want to be doing if you are going to enjoy the greatest possible success with your investments. Dollar cost-averaging, when implemented properly, will minimize the effects of these emotions.

Fundamental Analysis

With or without knowing it, almost all investors employ some type of fundamental analysis as they search out and select places to put their money. Some of these fundamentals include the state of the economy, corporate earnings, level of inflation, interest rates, and the political climate.

Fundamental analysts generally concern themselves with the reasons an investment proposition might look attractive. When applying this type of analysis in detail, you may not make a decision on an investment until you have pored over the balance sheets and income statements, read current and past annual reports, and made a thorough study of the business and financial outlook for the company in question, the industry in which it operates, and the state of U.S. and world economies.

Sources of information to do fundamental analysis are many. Data on earnings, sales, and other corporate financial matters can be obtained from annual and quarterly reports from the companies themselves, and from business and general-interest media. Data can also be obtained from publishers of financial information such as Standard & Poor's Corporation, Moody's Investors Service Inc., and Value Line, or from research reports issued by various brokerage firms.

You can use a computer to research the elaborate data bases available for extensive amounts of financial news and information. You can do a great deal of fundamental analysis at little or no cost if you have the time to devote to the subject. The financial section of your local library may offer a considerable amount of information at no cost to you.

The biggest problem in using fundamental analysis is, of course, to distinguish between information that is valuable and information that is not. Be careful when receiving information from full-service brokerage firms; the material may not always be strictly research material but may also be used as sales literature.

Technical Analysis

That clues to the future ups and downs of a given investment or market can be found in its past and present behavior is the primary assumption of technical analysis. Many technical analysts are purists who dismiss things like corporate-earnings estimates and interest-rate forecasts as distractions that are of no use in making investment decisions. Others follow the market and use a mixture of technical and fundamental analysis in helping them determine proper investment positioning.

The same places and people that can provide you with information regarding fundamental analysis can also provide you with information needed to do technical analysis. Many books have been written on both strategies. You may wish to look into the details of how each works and decide which one makes you most comfortable. Some combination of the two may be the answer for you.

Dividend-Reinvestment Plans

Benjamin Franklin once said, "Money makes money. And the money that money makes, makes more money."

Dividend-reinvestment plans allow shareholders to elect not to receive a check when dividends are paid periodically but instead to have the money automatically reinvested in additional shares of the fund or company involved. These plans provide a convenient means for long-term investors to build up their stock and/or mutual fund holdings with dividends they might otherwise spend. For the small investor, it makes possible the additional purchases of shares in small amounts. Many stockbrokers do not want to handle such small purchases or charge a prohibitive commission.

Once a dividend-reinvestment plan begins to operate, investments are made automatically and are reported on periodic statements issued to you by whatever entity handles the record keeping for the company or fund; often this is the company itself or an agent bank. Low cost is one of the most attractive features of dividend reinvestment plans. Some companies even offer a discount on the market price of the stock acquired through the dividend reinvestment. They do this to encourage participation in the plans, which provides them with a steady inexpensive supply of capital, and help create a loyal following of long-term share owners.

CHOOSING YOUR INVESTMENTS

The job of managing your own investments has grown much more complex in the last several years. The choices available to investors have multiplied at a rapid rate. People who once dealt with only passbook savings accounts, stocks, bonds, and a few other alternatives now are confronted with money market mutual funds, financial futures, stock index options, zero coupon bonds, adjustable rate securities, several new types of life insurance, and many other vehicles that did not exist, or were largely unknown to the public, just ten or 15 years ago.

This period of confusion and innovation occurred in part because inflation and fluctuations in interest rates changed the financial scene in the 1970s and early 1980s. Many of the new investments were created to meet the new needs and demands of people with money to manage. The modern menu of investment choices can present many opportunities to those who have the necessary knowledge to select wisely from them.

The following is a listing and description of some of the different investment vehicles that you might choose from when creating your own personal investment portfolio.

Central Assets Accounts

In the late 1970s, the investment firm of Merrill, Lynch, Pierce, Fenner & Smith introduced a multipurpose money management and investment vehicle known as the cash management account. It was designed to attract investors interested in consolidating their stock and bond trading, money market investing, and borrowing in a single account, covered by one monthly statement.

The financial institutions had their own reasons for liking these accounts. Such accounts enabled firms to build a solid customer base and provided a ready source of information about which of their customers were prime candidates for each of the financial services they provided.

No two central assets accounts are exactly alike. But all typically offer stock and bond brokerage service—full-service, discount, or both—a credit or debit card, ready access to credit through check writing, and an automatic sweep of any idle funds into an interest-bearing money market account. Some make available such extras as investment and tax-planning services.

Their great popularity is testimony to the appeal of central assets accounts. Before opening such an account, however, investors should consider whether the benefits to be gained will be worth the cost in fees. In particular, people who have trouble managing their use of credit should proceed carefully, since these accounts make it extremely easy to borrow as well as to save and invest.

Sponsors of central assets accounts typically charge an annual fee to cover their administrative costs in processing information for the accounts. In addition, your activities will still incur all the other standard costs. If you buy or sell securities, you will pay a brokerage commission. If you borrow money, you will be charged interest. It is important to determine how any individual institution sets its rates on these transactions and whether the rates would differ significantly from what you would pay if you managed your finances some other way.

Central assets accounts, by their very nature, are highly liquid. The cornerstone on which they are based—a money-market mutual fund or money-market deposit account—affords instant liquidity. In addition, they can facilitate the use of your money to best advantage by providing a convenient means of tapping any and all of your assets when an opportunity arises.

Annuities

Annuities are issued only by insurance companies, but they are marketed by a wide variety of institutions. You can find information at a securities brokerage firm or your local bank, as well as from specialized insurance salespeople.

The actual and potential costs of investing in an annuity can be complicated and should be kept in mind as you shop for one. Today, more and more annuities are available at no sales charge. But they may carry annual fees, charges and tax penalties for early withdrawal, and other costs. You should be aware of and understand all the cost provisions of an annuity before you invest.

Annuity sponsors normally set a minimum investment. In the case of deferred annuities, which permit you to accumulate money over time before you start receiving payments, this minimum is typically in the $1,000-to-$5,000 range.

A deferred annuity is one that does not start paying you money until some time after you buy it. It may call for a single premium investment at the time of purchase, or it may allow for many contributions after the initial investment is made.

Either way, the money in your account earns more money, which compounds until you withdraw it. What's more, the tax rules generally provide that the income is exempt from current taxes. This greatly accelerates the compounding process.

If you are willing to take on some extra risk during the accumulation period, you can invest in a variable annuity. In this kind of annuity, you can choose to have the premiums you pay in, and the money those premiums earn, invested in any one of several mutual funds, some of which may seek capital gains as an objective. Whatever course you choose to follow, the object is naturally to build up the largest possible amount in your account.

Bonds

The basic idea of a bond is simple. It is a security that represents a loan by the bond buyer to the bond issuer. The issuer (borrower) agrees to make periodic payments of interest to the buyer (lender) as long as the issuer has the use of the borrowed money, and to pay back the principal amount at an agreed-upon maturity date.

Investors in bonds need to be aware of how they differ from another major class of investments, stocks. A share of stock represents part ownership in an enterprise. A bond is merely a financial contract between two separate parties. It represents a claim on the assets of the issuer only in the event that the issuer is unable to live up to its part of the bargain. Should default occur, however, that claim comes ahead of stockholders' interests. This is why bonds are referred to as senior securities.

Almost all bonds are negotiable; that is, one investor can sell them to another at any time. There is a large secondary market for bonds, on stock exchanges and in the over-the-counter market, in which they are traded much like stocks.

Today the standard legal structure of bonds is the same as it always was. But the economic and financial circumstances that influence bonds has changed drastically, and so has the bond market. Large and sometimes rapid changes in inflation and interest rates have subjected bond prices to ups and downs.

Bonds may be bought and sold through brokers, banks, or dealers that specialize in a given segment of the market, such as municipal bonds. These organizations can provide you with abundant information about bonds.

There are many mutual funds, unit trusts, and closed-end funds that invest in bonds of all types. Information about these funds and trusts is available from the organizations that sponsor them or from brokers.

General-interest newspapers, financial publications, and investment advisory services report regularly on developments of interest to bond investors. Some specialized publications, news services, and advisory services devote all their attention to bonds.

Several companies, among them Moody's Investors Service Inc. and Standard & Poor's Corporation, evaluate the quality and safety of individual bond issues and assign them letter ratings from AAA (top quality) to D (in default). These can be used as guidelines in selecting a bond that most closely conforms to the degree of risk you want to take in quest of the highest possible return on your investment.

Bonds involve a variety of risks that require careful evaluation. The issuer can default. Or the price of even a top-quality bond may be ravaged by inflation and rising interest rates. Beyond these possibilities, bonds have some other inherent risks and drawbacks.

You may be required to sell a bond back to the issuer before maturity, either because it has been selected to go into a sinking fund (a method some bond issuers use to amass funds over time to pay off a bond issue at maturity) or because the entire issue has been called by the issuer. All sinking fund and call provisions should be understood before you invest in any given bond.

Furthermore, most bonds, unlike stocks, offer no hope of future increases in their payouts. With a straight bond, the interest rate is fixed for the life of the security. As inflation progresses, the purchasing power of this fixed payout will decline.

Corporate Bonds

Thousands of corporations raise capital in the United States by selling bonds. The two basic classes of these securities are mortgage bonds, which have the backing of a lien on some specified assets of the issuer, such as its production facilities; and debentures, which are backed by the issuer's "full faith and credit" but no specific assets. In theory, a bond may be a better credit risk than a debenture. But in practice, debentures of top-quality companies can and often do merit top credit standing.

The attraction of high-rated corporate bonds is that they usually offer higher yields than comparable government bonds at what most investment professionals regard as only a small increase in risk.

There are many subgroups within the broad category of corporate bonds. For purposes of evaluating them as credit risks, analysts distinguish industrial bonds from bonds issued by electric utilities, telephone companies, financial institutions, and finance companies. Specialized types of corporate bonds include equipment trust certificates issued by transportation companies, in which actual transportation equipment such as rail cars or aircraft serves as security for the loan.

If you have the skill or luck to buy a good corporate bond at a time when interest rates are at or near a peak, you can lock in attractive interest yields for long periods of time. Corporate bonds have been battered somewhat by inflation, but they still play a prominent role in income investing in this country.

Municipal Bonds

Municipals come in two basic categories: general obligation bonds and revenue bonds. General obligation issues are backed by the full financial power of the issuer, including its ability to set and collect taxes. Revenue bonds, by contrast, are typically backed only by the income expected from a given source for which the bond issue provides capital—for example, a toll highway or a sewer system. General obligation bonds are considered a better credit risk then revenue bonds, all other things being equal.

The presence of credit risk in municipal bonds was emphasized in investors' minds by the financial problems of New York City in the mid-1970s and the Washington Power Supply System (whose acronym led to the nickname "Whoops") in the early 1980s. Still, as a class of safe investments, municipals are generally ranked a bit below U.S. government securities and a bit above corporate bonds.

The primary appeal of municipal bonds for most individual investors is generous after-tax income. Whether they are a desirable way for you to pursue that goal depends on your individual tax bracket and prevailing market conditions.

Certificates of Deposit

Certificates of deposit (CDs) issued by banks and savings institutions play a major role in the U.S. financial system. They come in many forms and sizes, with maturities ranging from a few days or weeks to several years. There are jumbo CDs, in which institutions and professional investors may routinely invest millions of dollars. There are time deposit CDs, sometimes called savings certificates, which small investors may buy for as little as a few hundred dollars. No matter how it is structured, a CD is fundamentally a simple proposition—a loan of money by the buyer to a bank or savings institution for a specified period of time in return for interest on that money.

The dividing line that separates big CDs from small CDs is $100,000—the maximum amount of federal deposit insurance on principal and interest allowed for any single account with any single institution. If you invest more than $100,000 in a CD, you take some degree of credit risk—the chance that the issuer will fail or for some other reason be unable to make timely payments of principal and interest.

If you buy a small CD, by contrast, there is theoretically no credit risk, assuming that the federal deposit insurance agencies can fulfill their promise to cover any losses in any situation.

CDs are a primary money-management tool for savers and investors who want maximum income and safety from their assets. In periods of volatile interest rates, timing is of the essence in buying CDs. Ideally, you should have your money in a money-market deposit account, money market mutual fund, or very short term CD in periods when interest rates are rising. Just as rates hit their peak, you shift your money into a long-term CD, locking in a high return while yields on short-term investments begin to drop.

If this kind of thing were easy to do, many people would live in mansions and own yachts. Predicting interest-rate changes is a challenge that has defied the most knowledgeable and respected experts. You may count yourself fortunate and astute if you are even moderately successful in timing your investments in CDs.

Closed-End Funds

A close but little-known relative of the more common mutual funds are closed-end funds. They are sponsored by companies organized to pool their shareholders' money and invest in a portfolio of stocks, bonds, or both. Unlike mutual funds, however, closed-end funds do not continuously offer new shares to investors, nor do they stand ready to redeem shares for cash at any time of a shareholder's choosing. Instead, their shares are bought and sold on stock exchanges or in the over-the-counter market.

Some closed-end funds invest in a wide range of securities. Others confine themselves to specialities like bonds or securities of a single country.

Another variation on the same theme is the dual-purpose closed-end fund, which issues two classes of stock. One entitles the holder to all the dividend and interest income produced by the fund's portfolio; the other gives the holder a claim on all capital gains attained.

Brokers charge commissions to buy and sell closed-end funds, just as they do with other stocks. Investors who rely on their own research to make decisions about closed-end fund investments can seek to minimize commission costs by dealing with a discount broker.

As with a mutual fund, the return a closed-end fund can produce is reduced by the management fee charged by the fund's sponsor, which is paid periodically out of the fund's assets. Investors considering buying shares in a closed-end fund should familiarize themselves beforehand with all fees collected by the sponsor.

Closed-end funds specializing in bonds tend to offer yields comparable with those available in bonds and in bond mutual funds.

Commercial Paper

When an industrial corporation, finance company, bank-holding company, or state or local government wants to borrow money conveniently for a short period of time, it may sell commercial paper—a form of IOU. It may be backed by a bank line of credit or some other assurance, but it is not secured by any assets of the issuer.

Commercial paper is issued in maturities ranging from a few days to nine months, commonly on a discount basis. In this kind of arrangement, investors pay less than the face amount when they buy and receive the face amount at maturity, with the difference constituting the interest they receive.

A purchase of commercial paper from a direct issuer normally involves no costs other than telephone bills or postage. If, on the other hand, you buy through a banker or broker, you can expect to pay a commission or other transaction fee. This will effectively reduce the return you can expect on your investment.

In times of high short-term interest rates, commercial paper may offer attractive income prospects. When you are evaluating paper from this point of view, it makes sense to compare the return it offers with other competing vehicles like Treasury bills, bank and savings institution accounts, and money-market funds.

If you do not have the capital to diversify your commercial paper holdings and the time to monitor the money markets closely, you may find paper less attractive than, say, a bank savings certificate or government security. That holds particularly for investors who seek reliable long-term income, with absolute safety of principal, from their investments.

Commercial paper is generally considered a highly liquid investment, in the sense that it never involves tying up your funds for extended periods of time. However, it should be noted that there is no secondary market for paper; that is, there is no established place where an investor can readily sell it to someone else before maturity. If you find yourself in pressing need, an issuer may agree to buy it back from you before maturity.

Whenever you invest directly in commercial paper, you should select a maturity that fits your circumstances. This should be relatively simple, since a broad selection of maturities is normally available.

Common Stocks

No form of U.S. investment gets more attention and generates more emotion than common stocks.

The market has room for almost every kind of investor willing to take risks involved in part ownership of a business that may or may not thrive in the future. Some people try to trade stocks actively, playing the market. Others buy stocks of companies with promising prospects, holding them in hopes of long-term gains. Still others invest conservatively, buying stocks for the dividend income they produce and hoping that future dividend increases will help them keep pace with inflation.

Countless strategies, formulas, philosophies, and techniques have been developed over the years for trying to profit from investing in stocks. Using them, some people have been highly successful, while others, confronted with setback after setback, close out their brokerage accounts and vow "never again."

The quest for capital gains is the primary source of energy that drives the stock market. However, the higher you aim, the greater the risk of loss you must usually take.

You can choose to play conservatively in the stock market, choosing only stocks that historically have not fluctuated much in value and that pay a dividend large enough to cushion your capital from any modest decline in prices. But all common stocks expose you to the likelihood of some degree of capital gain or loss. With changes in business and economic conditions, today's conservative stock can become tomorrow's high-risk issue.

With the very active markets that operate in this country, stocks as a class of investments are considered very liquid. In usual circumstances, stocks can readily be bought and sold on short notice. This liquidity varies from stock to stock, however, depending on the amount of activity that takes place with it. A stock that consistently makes the active list on the New York Stock Exchange is regarded as much more liquid than a tiny, unknown over-the-counter issue.

Stocks that have relatively few shares in public hands are often described as "thinly" traded. In issues like this, the price changes from one transaction to another can be considerable.

Preferred Stocks

Preferred stocks are securities, like common stocks, that represent part ownership of a corporation. They are described as preferred because they have the first right, before common stocks, to any money the corporation has available to pay out in dividends.

While a preferred issue's dividend is generally more secure than a common stock, it is usually fixed. For that reason, a straight preferred stock tends to behave more like a bond.

But as a stock, it lacks some of the most important legal characteristics of a bond. When a company gets into trouble, investors who own its debt securities, such as bonds, normally have a claim on the company's assets. At the very least, they stand first in line to get allotments of whatever is left should the company be liquidated. Preferred stockholders in such situations remain owners, not creditors, of the company.

There are many details to consider in evaluating a preferred stock: voting rights, call provisions, sinking funds, cumulative arrangements for unpaid dividends, and more. Any and all of these can significantly affect the way the market values a preferred stock.

You can invest in nonconvertible preferred stocks seeking capital gains. However, several factors that differ from the usual forces at work with common stocks influence their prices. One primary reason for buying common stocks is the hope of future dividend increases. This hope does not exist with preferred stocks.

Since preferred stocks are held mainly by income-conscious investors, the ups and downs of interest rates tend to exert a strong influence on prices of preferred stocks. Like bonds, preferred stocks generally fall in value when interest rates rise and increase in value when rates decline. The market for common stocks may also be influenced by changes in interest rates, but there the effect is less uniform and may be mitigated by other developments.

The main appeal of preferred stocks is their dividend yield. Before buying a preferred stock for income, however, you should consider your tax status and the many alternatives available, such as, perhaps, an outstanding bond of the same company.

Convertible Securities

Many corporations have issued convertible preferred stocks or convertible debentures (commonly referred to as convertible bonds). These securities carry a fixed interest or dividend rate but may be exchanged whenever their owners wish—subject to any limits spelled out by the issuer—for a specified amount of common stock. As a result of their dual character, convertibles can provide their owners with fairly generous income, while at the same time giving them the hope of benefiting from rising stock prices.

They also may at times provide a degree of protection from adverse market conditions. If the price of a company's common stock declines, the conversion value of its convertibles will drop too. But, in theory at least, the comparatively high yield of the convertible may act as a brake on any sharp decline in its price.

Investors should differentiate between convertible securities that are debentures and those that are preferred stocks. Debentures are debt issues that rank ahead of any preferred or common stocks as claims on the assets of the issuer. In addition, dividends paid on preferred stocks are largely free of tax to corporations that own the shares but not to individual investors. This has the effect of making preferreds somewhat less attractive to individuals than competing fixed-income securities, all other things being equal.

Most, but not all, convertibles are issued with the common stock of the issuer as the underlying security.

Although convertible securities usually offer higher yields than common stocks of the same issuer, they also usually offer lower yields than you could obtain on straight debt securities that have no conversion features. Therefore, they may not be especially attractive for investors whose paramount objective is maximum current income from their assets. Straight fixed-income investments, of course, offer no protection from inflation. With a convertible, there is the hope of a rise in the price of the underlying common stock and thus some chance of at least partial protection from inflation.

Credit Unions

In an era of rapid financial change, credit unions retain an old-fashioned appeal for many savers, investors, and borrowers. They are nonprofit cooperatives, owned by their members.

Credit unions have traditionally provided a convenient place to save and at the same time are a source of readily available credit, usually at attractive interest rates. Credit unions can provide these services because their costs tend to be very low (and because they are normally not subject to federal taxation).

Members of any credit union must share some common bond. That bond is most commonly related to their work, but credit unions can also be organized by people who live in the same community or belong to the same religious organization or fraternal or civic group.

All federal credit unions, and nearly all state-chartered credit unions, are covered by deposit insurance, usually up to $100,000 per account. However, in a few states, state-chartered credit unions are not required by law to be covered by this insurance. It makes good sense to inquire about its insurance arrangement before joining any credit union. At the same time, you may also ask what insurance, if any, the credit union provides or sells to cover loan balances in the event that you die or become disabled.

Liquidity can be one of the prime selling points of a good, insured credit union. A credit union at your place of work can be an ideal place to keep funds you may need to tap at short notice. Loans may be available without processing or qualifying delays. Of course, if you invest in something other than a standard savings vehicle at your credit union, the liquidity of your assets may be affected.

Limited Partnerships

In limited partnership investments, the firm that organizes and sells the venture typically names itself or an affiliate as the sole general partner. It then offers a piece of the action to limited partners as units.

Some limited partnerships are referred to as private. They are not registered with the Securities and Exchange Commission (SEC) and generally are sold only to small numbers of wealthy investors. Public limited partnerships, by contrast, are registered with and reviewed by the SEC. However, "reviewed" does not mean "approved."

Public partnerships are offered in pieces as small as a few thousand dollars. They are even marketed for use in individual retirement accounts and other tax-favored savings programs. Whether public or private, limited partnerships may offer attractions that are hard to find elsewhere. But they also involve special risks that should be carefully evaluated and understood before you invest.

The costs of investing in limited partnerships are generally high. Large up-front sales charges are common, and the general partner often collects a variety of fees once the venture is in operation. You should have a thorough understanding of all the fees you will, or might, be charged before you invest.

Some limited partnerships take substantial risks in the hope of achieving large capital gains. Some realize this goal; others do not. When people evaluate a partnership's prospects, they generally look into the sponsor's past record in similar programs. But, of course, past successes are no assurance of future ones.

In the process of evaluating a partnership investment, it is possible to get so preoccupied with all the trappings of the deal—its structure, potential tax benefits, and so on—that you overlook the fundamental business questions: Does the whole venture make economic sense? Is the price right? If you were a wealthy investor operating on your own, would you consider making the same commitment?

Conservative investors who want or need maximum income and safety of principal generally should not expect a limited partnership to offer the protection from risk available with such vehicles as Treasury bills or federally insured deposits.

As a general rule, limited partnerships are moderate-to-high-risk propositions. There have been cases when even large, well-respected sponsors of these packages have failed to deliver expected returns because of adverse business developments. There have also been highly publicized cases of outright fraud.

In addition, it is important to understand that, as a limited partner, you have little or no say in how a venture operates once you invest. In real estate, for example, it is common for units to be sold before the syndicate even has decided what properties to buy. Because of their illiquidity, limited partnerships are generally not a suitable place for money you might want or need before the time when they are scheduled to be dissolved.

Master Limited Partnerships

An exception to that general rule of illiquidity in limited partnerships arose when some independent oil and gas companies decided to consolidate various limited partnerships they managed into single "master" limited partnerships (MLPs). Units of these larger entities qualified for listing on stock exchanges or for trading in the over-the-counter market. Suddenly, here was an investment that combined many of the advantages of a partnership with some of the attributes of a stock. From the energy industry, the idea spread to real estate, other types of commodity businesses, health care, agriculture, cable television, and beyond.

MLPs gave investors the chance to invest in partnerships in the hope of realizing trading profits.

Even more important, many MLPs were able to make distributions to investors that were not immediately subject to income tax, since they were considered a return of those investors' original capital. And if there were taxable distributions, some or all of them could be sheltered by a pass-through of tax deductions for such things as depreciation and operating expenses.

To the extent that a MLP functioned as a tax shelter, creating passive losses for its investors that they could write off against their other income, the Tax Reform Act of 1986 reduced the tax advantages the partnership could offer.

At least two important categories of costs must be considered when you are contemplating an investment in an MLP. One is the management and operating costs collected by the general partner. The other is the commission you can expect to pay—either explicitly stated or built into the price—when you buy or sell through a broker. This commission may be less than the sales charge imposed on some old-style conventional limited partnerships. On the other hand, it may be more than you would have to pay on some newer partnerships, designed as conservative income-producing investments.

Many MLPs are set up to offer attractive current returns. The yield figure on MLPs can be misleading, however. If you receive a payment that is offset for tax purposes by depreciation charges or is declared to be a return of capital, you do not escape taxation on it—you merely postpone the tax liability. Both depreciation and return of capital payments reduce your cost basis, the amount you subtract from the price you receive when you sell or cash in your investment to determine the amount of capital gain on which you must pay tax. Of course, under the new tax bill, long-term gains are no longer given special tax treatment.

Furthermore, a return of capital should not be thought of as yield at all. If a financial operator takes $100 of your money and then returns $10 to you six months later, reducing your position in the enterprise in question to $90, your "yield" is zero.

The trappings of master limited partnerships may confuse some fundamental issues for investors, especially if investors are not thoroughly familiar with the ways in which these vehicles operate. Whatever structural characteristics they may have that differ from stocks, MLPs generally can succeed only if they are based on sound business plans and operate in a favorable economic climate.

Mortgage Securities

Typically, a mortgage-backed security is created when an agent gathers together a large package of loans, then cuts the package up again into pieces for sale to investors. The investors thereafter receive their proportionate share of the interest payments on the mortgages and the principal payments as well.

Three big names in the business are government-fostered companies and agencies known as the Federal Home Loan Mortgage Corporation, the Federal National Mortgage Association, and the Government National Mortgage Association. They are usually referred to by the nicknames Freddie Mac, Fannie Mae, and Ginnie Mae, respectively. Other private agents with no links to the government are appearing in increasing numbers.

Most mortgage securities are known as pass-throughs, because the packager passes through monthly interest and principal payments directly to investors. A newer variation, which met with an enthusiastic initial response, is the collateralized mortgage obligation, a corporate bond backed by mortgages that typically makes payments of interest semiannually.

Prices of interest-bearing investments, including mortgage securities, move up and down in opposite direction from shifts in the prevailing level of interest rates. Thus, it is possible to realize a capital gain from a mortgage security after a period of falling interest rates. However, mortgage securities are aimed primarily at investors for a generous yield, not capital gains.

In the past, mortgage securities have offered returns higher than Treasury bonds of comparable maturity without any major sacrifice of safety or liquidity.

With many types of mortgage securities, some confusion is possible about periodic payments that investors receive. When homeowners make their monthly mortgage payments, they pay interest and a portion of the principal amount of their loans. Frequently, they pay off the loan well before their scheduled maturity dates when they sell their houses and move.

The way many mortgage securities are set up, payments to investors also are part interest, part principal. Investors in these securities must be aware that the checks they are receiving represent not just earnings on their investments but also a partial return of the money they put up in the first place.

This arrangement is fine with some investors, while others find it unwieldy. The problem can be averted if an investor selects a mortgage security, unit trust, or mutual fund that provides for automatic and immediate reinvestment of the principal payments received in new mortgages. Some also provide for reinvestment of interest payments if the investor does not wish to receive them as current income.

Mutual Funds

Mutual funds are companies organized to pool and invest money received from shareholders, providing benefits such as convenience and diversification that individuals might not be able to obtain through direct investment in stocks, bonds, and other securities.

The various types of mutual funds share some important common characteristics. They are generally open-ended; that is, they stand ready every business day to sell new shares directly to investors and to redeem old shares for investors who wish to cash them in. One exception to the rule occurs occasionally when a fund opts to suspend sales of shares to new investors.

The price of a mutual fund is set daily by its net asset value per share—the total worth of its investments and other assets divided by the number of shares outstanding.

So-called load funds marketed through salespeople or brokers impose a sales charge of up to 8.5 percent of the amount you put up when you invest. They usually set sliding scales under which the percentage charge decreases gradually as the size of the investment increases. A relatively new breed, called low-load, carries a smaller sales charge of perhaps two to four percent.

No-load funds, by contrast, collect no such commission and boast that 100 percent of the money you entrust them with goes to work for you.

In any case, no fund is free of all costs. The investment advisors that operate them collect an annual management fee from the fund's assets. This is usually a percentage—say, 0.5 percent—of the total average assets in the fund over the period in question. You never have to pay this fee out of your pocket, but it has the effect of diminishing the return you get on your investment.

Another fee imposed by some funds is known as a 12b-1 charge, after the regulatory rule that applies to them. It is collected from the assets of the fund to cover distribution costs on the sale of new fund shares. This practice has produced much criticism, and the rule covering it may well be changed in the future.

Your chances of realizing capital gains depend on what kind of fund you choose. Some funds investing in stocks concentrate on smaller companies or speculative special situations. They often show dramatic gains in rising markets, but they may also be the worst performers of all when the stock market is falling. From these aggressive growth funds, the emphasis on capital gains theoretically decreases in steps through several categories: growth funds, balanced funds, income funds, and money market funds. Money-market funds, which invest in short-term interest-bearing securities, usually follow a policy of holding their net asset values stable while paying out regular interest income and thus offer little or no hope of capital gains.

Over long periods of time, the top-performing funds have compiled outstanding records of capital gains. Among the hundreds of other funds available are others that have shown only fair or even poor results.

As with capital gains, the potential for income from mutual funds varies with the objective of the fund and the skill of its management. Some, such as bond and money-market funds, offer yields that are competitive with other investments aimed at income-conscious investors. Aggressive growth funds, by contrast, typically offer current yields that range from small to negligible. This is by design, since their emphasis is on capital appreciation, and many of their shareholders have no interest in obtaining current income.

By comparison with many other types of investments, mutual funds are generally highly liquid. Except under extraordinary circumstances described in the prospectus, they stand ready to sell or redeem shares for cash at short notice. In recent years, increasing numbers of funds have established services that allow the owner of the fund to redeem shares instantly by simply writing a check.

Many investors nowadays judge their funds not only by investment results but also by the services that they offer and how well they perform those services. With the wide array of no-load funds to choose from in today's market, there is no need to keep your money in a fund whose shareholder services are consistently poor.

Growth Funds

One of the biggest and broadest categories of mutual funds comes under the general heading of growth funds. These funds seek appreciation of their shareholders' assets, employing any one of an almost limitless number of strategies in the stock market.

The best growth funds have achieved handsome results for their investors over long periods of time. Occasionally, some growth funds run up dramatic gains in short periods as well. When this happens, enthusiasm for the most venturesome funds runs high, and investors typically pour new money into them in huge amounts. Recent history has shown that these circumstances amount to a danger signal—a sign that a bull market (one hopeful of rising prices) in stocks and stock funds may be approaching its peak.

There are two ways of realizing capital gains in growth funds. To avoid incurring a tax obligation, funds must pass through to their shareholders gains the funds achieve when they sell securities. These are called capital gains distributions. Fund investors may elect to accept these distributions in cash or to have them automatically reinvested in new fund shares. Most investors pursuing long-term growth opt for automatic reinvestment.

At the same time, fund shareholders hope that the prices of stock still held in their fund's portfolio will rise, increasing the fund's net asset value per share; this value is calculated daily. Unlike the capital gains distribution, over which the individual fund shareholder has little or no control, this kind of capital gain is realized at the investor's discretion, when he or she chooses to redeem shares of the fund.

Funds that aim for the greatest possible capital gains also tend to involve the greatest risk of losses. If any growth fund is poorly run or operates in a period of adverse market conditions, there is always the chance that an investor will realize no capital gains of any kind.

Balanced Funds

Some mutual fund investors have more than one goal. They may, for example, want both fairly generous income from their savings and the hope of protecting those savings from inflation by means of capital appreciation. Such investors may look to a fund that seeks these dual objectives, which may be described as a growth and income fund or balanced fund.

Balanced funds do offer conservative investors a sort of compromise alternative to making a choice between the stock market and the bond market. In a sense, they are roughly the mutual fund equivalent of a convertible bond—and, in fact, a given balanced fund may well invest in convertibles.

Typically, balanced funds offer yields that exceed the income available from growth funds but that fall short of current returns offered by straight income funds and other high-yielding investments. The income produced by a balanced fund can provide some cushion against whatever market risks the fund takes.

Balanced funds enjoy the high liquidity offered by most types of mutual fund investments. They have traditionally been a popular choice for investors who want to enroll in withdrawal plans. Under these plans, investors elect to receive regular periodic payments from their fund accounts, hoping that dividends, interest, and capital gains—however irregularly realized—will cover the payments received over time. For investors like these, and indeed for many others, volatility of interest rates and the bond market is an unwelcome development.

Sector Funds

While most funds are promoted on the fundamental precept of diversification, sector funds were designed to be just the opposite; they are concentrated in a single group of stocks.

The funds are not necessarily operated for the conservative, long-term investor but rather for the active trader looking for chances to earn above-average profits and willing to take above-average risks. Instead of taking a flier in a single high-technology stock, for example, the trader might buy a high-tech sector fund, thereby avoiding the need to pay brokerage commissions on both purchase and sale.

To invest in a sector fund, you must have great confidence in your sense of timing. Too often, the record shows, enthusiasm for any given sector fund is likely to peak just as, or after, the stocks it owns top out and lapse into disfavor.

Most sector funds are designed for investors who are willing to assume considerable risk in the hope of realizing large capital gains, perhaps in shorter periods of time than with a diversified fund.

Some families of funds offer a wide menu of sector funds with convenient arrangements for switching your money from one portfolio to another. This presupposes that you have some talent for anticipating when today's hot stock groups will turn cold and which other groups will subsequently rise to take their place. If you have this ability, or just plain luck, you are in a distinct minority in the population of investors.

Most sector funds are no place to put your money if you want or need a reliable, stable flow of income from your assets. The problem is not just their volatility; many sector funds concentrate on stocks of young, growing industries, where dividends tend to be low or nonexistent.

International Funds

There are three distinct types of international funds. One category invests exclusively in foreign markets, a second may divide its money between foreign and U.S. securities, and the last concentrates in a single country or region of the world. Many single-country investment companies are set up as closed-end funds. One way in which you might set up your own international portfolio would be to own a diversified sampling of these funds.

If you contemplate investing in a single-country fund, obviously it would be wise to have some knowledge of that country's economy, financial system, and political situation.

Many international funds have capital gains as their primary investment objective. Some international funds seek income in the form of dividends and interest from foreign securities, especially those traded in countries where prevailing yields are higher than yields in the U.S. markets. Such a fund may represent an attractive proposition for investors who are aware of, and prepared to assume, the risks involved. If interest rates are higher in some other nation than they are in the United States, it makes sense to question why that is so. Is that country's economy plagued by some special problem? If so, does that problem threaten to jeopardize future dividend and interest payments?

An international fund may be ideally suited for a venturesome investor willing to take some chances in order to get a better return. At the same time, it may merit considerable caution for anyone who wants or needs maximum safety along with income to meet basic living expenses.

Income Funds

A fund can assemble a portfolio of bonds, other fixed-income securities, high-yielding common stocks, or any combination thereof, and sell part interests in that portfolio to individual investors in the form of shares of the fund. In this way, investors can participate in a diversified package of income-producing investments that reduces their exposure to risk of default or a dividend reduction or elimination by any single issuer.

As managed portfolios of securities with varying maturities, mutual funds for income have no set maturity date of their own. As a result, interest-rate risk has become a constant factor in evaluating the investment merits of any given fund.

For their income funds to perform well, fund managers must not only choose investments that offer attractive yields in relation to credit risk, but they must also choose those investments at the right time and in the right maturities. In order to achieve the best results on their investments, people who invest in income funds must also be skillful, or lucky, in the timing of their decisions to buy and redeem shares of the funds.

Many types of longer-term income funds are available today. Some take a broad approach, trying to maximize their holdings of long-term securities when interest rates appear likely to decline and to take cover in less vulnerable money-market securities when they foresee a rise in interest rates. Others focus on a single specific objective—high yield, say, or high quality. As long as interest rates remain volatile, however, investments in income funds will be exposed at least to some extent to the ups and downs of a difficult market.

Interest-rate risk may be an unpleasant fact of life for many investors. But it does carry with it the possibility of capital gains in times when rates decline.

Before you buy an income fund in quest of capital gains, there are several questions to be asked: Do you strongly believe that interest rates are headed lower? Is the fund you have in mind in a position to gain maximum advantage from such a drop? How long are you willing to wait to see if your expectations are fulfilled?

Some funds take an aggressive, high-risk approach to investing in bonds and similar vehicles. They may employ timing strategies, or they may climb out on the limb of credit risk, buying so-called junk bonds (bonds with high interest *and* high risk). Such funds are not suitable for, nor designed for, investors concerned primarily with reliable, steady income from their assets.

In times when inflation accelerates and interest rates rise, just about all investors in high-yielding securities suffer in one way or another. Owners of fixed investments like bonds or bond-unit trusts have a choice in how they accept their financial misfortune. They can confront their losses directly, selling their existing holdings at a depressed price and putting what remains of the money into newer, higher-yielding vehicles. Or they can hold on, waiting to receive the face value at maturity—but letting inflation continue to erode the purchasing power of their money in the meantime.

Under these same conditions, owners of an income mutual fund face a different set of circumstances. Shares of an income fund do not have a face, or maturity, value. Their only value is the net asset value, which is recalculated daily to reflect all that has occurred.

Managers of income funds take active steps to try to limit losses in bad markets and reap the greatest possible benefit from rising ones. Your assessment of a given income fund may hinge largely on whether you believe the fund's managers can indeed succeed in the task.

Municipal Bond Funds

As long as the credit markets in general, and the municipal bond market in particular, remain volatile, a well-timed investment in a well-managed municipal bond fund may produce capital gains to go with attractive tax-favored income.

However, the primary goal of a typical municipal bond fund is to realize the highest possible after-tax income for its investors consistent with the amount of risk they are willing to take. Credit risk (the ability to pay off debt) can vary greatly among municipal bond issues. So some funds may concentrate on lower-quality issues in quest of the greatest possible yield, while others may emphasize quality and concede a few points in yield. What this means for the conservative investor is that the highest-yielding fund might not be the most desirable investment.

The key question for any yield-conscious investor, of course, is the after-tax return available on alternative investments. A broker or fund sponsor can provide you with tables useful in determining whether, in your tax bracket, a taxable fund or a tax-free fund best fits your circumstances.

Before investing in a municipal bond fund, or any other tax-favored investment, it makes sense to calculate whether you are giving up more in potential return from alternative vehicles than you are gaining in tax breaks.

Money-Market Funds

A money-market fund is organized along the classic lines of a mutual fund. Fund sponsors put a pool of money to work, distributing the proceeds it earns to the fund's shareholders. Instead of stocks or bonds, however, money funds invest only in short-term securities in the credit markets—Treasury bills, large bank certificates of deposit, commercial paper, banker's acceptances (promissory notes), or any other kind of low-risk, high-yielding security of relatively short duration that comes along.

Some money funds confine themselves to a single category, such as government securities or commercial paper. Others hold a mixture. While nearly all money funds operate in similar ways and are considered safe investments as a general rule, there are gradations of risk and variances in yield from fund to fund.

A money fund should never be confused with a bank investment (the rough equivalent in banking is the money-market deposit account).

Money funds may be used as a convenient, temporary parking place for idle funds—to keep money at work when it is not invested elsewhere.

Generous current income is a primary attraction of money funds in periods when interest rates are high. Since no two funds have precisely identical portfolios, their yields may vary considerably. Many financial publications and newspapers publish weekly tables of individual funds' recent yields. You can normally get a current figure on any fund by telephoning the fund itself.

An important point to bear in mind is that money fund yields usually follow, but lag behind, interest rate trends. That is so because the amount of interest the fund can earn changes only as securities in portfolio mature and are replaced with new ones offering different interest rates. The length of this time lag for a given fund depends on the average maturity in its portfolio.

Ideally, an investor wants to have money in a very short-term fund when rates are rising and in a fund with a relatively long average maturity when rates are falling. Some sophisticated investors and institutions invest directly in the money markets in periods of stable or rising interest rates, but move into money funds when rates are declining to take advantage of the funds' lag time.

One reason for the great popularity of money funds is the exceptional liquidity they provide. Most offer a broad selection of methods by which you can redeem shares at any time, including unlimited check writing for amounts of $500 or more per check (lower with some funds). There is no guarantee that every fund will always be so liquid in the future. But it is reasonable to expect that well-managed funds run by reputable sponsors will continue to offer this advantage, even in turbulent economic times.

NOW and Super-NOW Accounts

Earn interest on your checking account!

That alluring prospect became a reality with the idea of NOW (negotiable order of withdrawal) accounts. Negotiable orders of withdrawal functioned exactly like checks and for all-but-technical legal purposes were, in fact, checks. But, in contrast with the standard checking account, the bank or savings institution paid interest on the balance of your NOW account.

At first, the maximum interest rate was limited to 5.25 percent. Then regulators of banks and savings institutions, at about the same time they created money-market deposit accounts in the early 1980s, authorized what came to be called Super-NOW accounts.

With Super-NOW accounts, banks and savings institutions were given the right to pay whatever interest rate they chose on balances over $2,500. This minimum was lowered by stages to zero as of January 1, 1986. But more financial institutions continued to set their own minimums, often in the $2,500 range, below which they paid only low or no interest.

Unlike money-market deposit accounts (MMDAs), Super-NOW Accounts allow for unlimited check writing. In practice, many institutions have designed their Super-NOWs along the lines of a traditional checking rather than a savings account. For example, they may be offered with debit cards (a plastic substitute for a checkbook) and automatic lines of credit.

NOWs and Super-NOWs provide a way to gain income from your assets by earning interest on money you keep available for ready use. In that sense, they represent a potential improvement from the saver's point of view over older forms of checking accounts. However, rates offered even on Super-NOWs may not be competitive with those available on money-market mutual funds. In addition, the net income you realized from a NOW or Super-NOW may be reduced by fees and service charges incurred in your use of the account.

Rates paid on Super-NOWs, like those on MMDAs, are subject to change monthly or even more frequently. When you are shopping for a Super-NOW, it makes sense to inquire how any given institution calculates the rate it will pay.

NOWs and Super-NOWs are considered highly liquid. In fact, they have a slight liquidity edge over MMDAs, in that they permit you to write checks and make other third-party payments from them as frequently as you wish.

Their liquidity is flawed, however, by some of the rules covering them. As long as there is a minimum balance required for access to top interest rates, that amount of money is effectively frozen as long as you wish to gain the advantages of those rates. Also, some institutions may impose service charges when your balance falls below specified levels, which has the effect of limiting your options on your use of the money in a NOW or Super-NOW account.

Passbook Savings Accounts

Many millions of dollars are still on deposit in passbook savings accounts. Many people still use them for short-term savings goals. Parents still choose them as a handy way to introduce their children to the virtues of saving. But by many standards—including potential growth or income, flexibility, and tax status—passbook accounts in their present form are an idea whose time has passed.

They are outclassed in yield by a wide variety of vehicles that are considered just as safe, or even safer. Even though they provide banks and savings institutions with a seemingly cheap source of money, many of those cost-burdened institutions have lately taken steps to reduce the appeal of small passbook accounts.

As long as no active steps are taken to kill it off, a phenomenon as deeply rooted in American society as the passbook savings account seems unlikely to disappear from the scene any time soon. In the modern, highly competitive world, however, it will have to develop some new attractions if it is going to have a chance to thrive again.

Opening a passbook savings account has always been a relatively simple process at any bank or savings institution. If you seek to open one these days, any conscientious banker will advise you of the many other alternatives available at no sacrifice in safety and, in some cases, at not much sacrifice in liquidity.

Passbook savings accounts are interest-bearing vehicles. But people who want or need maximum current income from their investments, perhaps more than any other class of investors, should be aware of the many, more appealing alternatives not only in other types of bank deposits but also in Treasury securities and other very low-risk vehicles.

Passbook savings accounts are highly liquid. True, you can't write a check on one, as you can with a money-market deposit account, NOW or Super-NOW account, or money-market fund. But the money is there for ready withdrawal in person, by mail, and increasingly these days, by telephone transfers into, say, your checking account at the same bank for immediate use elsewhere.

Precious Metals

If money is defined as a store of value and a medium of exchange, some investors consider precious metals the ultimate form of money.

So precious metals have evolved as separate investments, whose prices fluctuate regularly—and sometimes wildly—when stated in dollars or any other paper currency. Some investors put a great deal of trust in gold and silver as a repository of value that offers protection from the ills that can befall paper currencies: inflation, political instability, and changing values of currencies relative to one another in foreign exchange. In the view of some people, currencies have only relative value, while gold and silver are absolutes, or very nearly so.

Another commodity, platinum, has a shorter history in the realm of money and finance. But many people today classify it with gold and silver as precious metal.

The means and methods available for investing in precious metals today are almost limitless. You can buy gold, silver or platinum in the form of bullion (bars of various weights). You can buy gold and silver coins. You can buy the stock of companies that mine or process precious metals or shares of mutual funds that invest in these stocks. You can trade options or futures contracts that represent an interest in gold, silver, or platinum.

Many strategies are available for seeking capital gains in precious metals. Typically, investors look to precious metals first and foremost as a hedge against inflation. They buy for the long term, trusting that the value of gold or silver or platinum will rise at least enough to keep up with increases in the cost of living.

Real Estate

In modern real estate investing, you can pursue almost any strategy you wish, whether it is speculative or conservative, long-term or short-term. You can buy somebody else's package or put together your own.

The investment possibilities of real estate are endless and, when properly handled, profitable. However, real estate can be expensive to buy, own, and sell. The ownership costs can be substantial and unpredictable. In direct real estate investment, costs include property taxes, insurance, maintenance, and repairs. The investment can consume considerable time and money. If you can't or don't want to accommodate yourself to this prospect, you can hire someone to handle it. But, of course, paying that person will be another cost.

You can keep your out-of-pocket expenses to a minimum by investing, say, in the stock of a company that in turn owns real estate. That arrangement makes you a part owner of an entity that may pay large real estate costs, but you still may see a large return on your investments. Some types of real estate investments—in particular, a personal

residence—offer attractive tax breaks that lighten the burden of ownership costs.

Many investors take the plunge into real estate in hopes of realizing
handsome capital gains—whether they buy undeveloped swampland or a
condominium in a high rise.

However, there are a good many ways to invest in real estate with the
primary objective of income, for example: in selected real estate limited
partnerships or in real estate investment trusts. There are other strategies
for combined income and capital gains goals, for example: buying a developed property that yields generous rental income while the value of
the property appreciates.

Another approach among the almost-limitless possibilities in real estate is to buy a multi-unit property, such as a two-family house, in which
you occupy one of the units and rent out the other. The standard aim in
such a situation is to use the rental income from tenants to help cover
your costs of both owning and occupying the property.

However, for the conservative investor concerned not only with de-
pendable income but also with liquidity and maximum safety of principal, most real estate investments fall behind alternatives such as U.S.
government securities.

Real estate is inherently illiquid. Depending on the market, it is sometimes difficult to sell quickly, and especially when circumstances indicate
that you *must* sell it quickly. This poor liquidity rule is generally true but
is not an ironclad absolute.

Real Estate Investment Trusts

Real estate as an investment traditionally suffers two drawbacks. It is generally inaccessible to people with only a few hundred or few thousand
dollars to invest. And real estate investments are illiquid, especially if an
owner is forced to sell on short notice.

To counter these problems, the real estate investment trust (REIT) was
developed. A REIT is an enterprise that gathers together money from
many investors and invests that money in real estate properties, real estate loans, or both. A REIT resembles a mutual fund in that it holds a diversified portfolio of investments and distributes substantially all the
income it earns in the form of dividends to shareholders. Unlike mutual
funds, however, REITs are not open-ended—that is, they don't constantly stand ready to issue new shares to investors. Instead, their shares
trade like other common stocks on stock exchanges or in the over-the-
counter market.

Whatever their merits, REITs do not constitute a direct investment in real estate. Rather, their shares represent part ownership of a real estate investment enterprise. Decisions about how, when, and where to invest in real estate are made by the management of the company. The results a REIT investor achieves depend on the dividend income the management is able to earn for shareholders and on what value the market places on the shares of the REIT.

A relatively new form of REIT is the self-liquidating trust. This type of trust states its intention, at the time it is organized, of selling all its holdings; distributing the proceeds to shareholders; and dissolving at a specified future date, or possibly earlier at the discretion of management.

Liquidity is a prime selling point of REITs. It might take you months to find the right house, for example, and months to sell it again later. By contrast, REIT shares can normally be bought and sold in a matter of a few minutes, whenever you choose, with a telephone call or a visit to a broker's office. They provide investors who have a feel for the national economy with a means to move their money in and out of the real estate market whenever they believe the time is right to do so.

Repurchase Agreements

A repurchase agreement, or repo, can be viewed as a form of loan, the interest on which is the difference between the price the lender pays to buy on date X and the price received on date Y. Its actual legal status may be much more complicated than that. But assuming that the repurchase agreement is carried out as agreed upon, one party has effectively employed it to gain the use of another party's money in return for payment resembling interest.

Some money-market funds, including those with a policy of using only government securities, make a regular practice of buying repos. Others do not, preferring to limit themselves to direct ownership of Treasury bills.

Lenders such as money-market mutual funds sometimes regard repos as an appealing way to invest for income. With repos, they may be able to keep the maturity of their portfolios very short so as to retain maximum flexibility in their investment strategy in times when they are concerned about the outlook for interest rates. Often these funds can obtain a higher yield for their shareholders than funds investing all their assets directly in government securities. When the buyer and seller, at the time a repo is created, set a stated price for the completion of the transaction, they also effectively set a fixed interest rate for a period in which other open-market interest rates are subject to frequent fluctuations.

In day-to-day practice, repos of the kind normally bought by money funds are considered very liquid. In fact, the money funds and other institutions that deal in them may use them as a tool to maintain a high degree of flexibility and liquidity in their money management strategies. The government-guaranteed Treasury bills that stand behind them contribute to this liquidity.

However, repos themselves are not guaranteed by the government. So in times of strain in the credit markets, the liquidity of a given repos may be significantly affected by the way it is legally written, by court rulings, and/or by the financial soundness and integrity of the individual or institution that originated it.

U.S. Government Securities

There is no such thing as a risk-free investment. But among the countless entities around the world to which you can entrust your money, the government of the United States is generally considered the safest bet by far. U.S. government securities represent the ultimate in quality.

Because the government is so big and so prone to borrowing, these securities are available in vast amounts. You can put your money in them for periods as short as a few days or as long as nearly thirty years. You can invest as little as $25 in a savings bond, or millions in another kind of government instrument.

Although the various types of government securities are all nominally interest-paying vehicles, each type has distinctive characteristics. The main types are Treasury bonds and notes, Treasury bills, government agency securities, and savings bonds.

There are many mutual funds, unit trusts, and other packaged pools of money that invest in government securities. Some are specifically set up to invest only in government securities.

Government securities are a prime candidate for any investor who wants a combination of current income and maximum safety. Because of their high credit standing, however, government securities usually offer somewhat lower yields than those available on debt securities of other issuers, even solid blue-chip corporations.

In assessing the relative risks and rewards of various debt securities, investors who live in states and localities that levy taxes on interest income should keep in mind that interest on government securities is exempt from state and local taxation.

Most government securities (with the exception of savings bonds in the first few years after purchase) are highly liquid. In cases where the government does not stand ready to redeem them for you, you can usually expect to find large numbers of willing buyers and sellers in the secondary market.

If you have a sum of money that you expect to need soon but that you wish to keep at work in the interim, Treasury bills or a money-market mutual fund specializing in short-term government securities may suit your needs very well.

U.S. Savings Bonds

The basic U.S. savings bond sold is the Series EE bond, which carries an interest rate that floats up and down based on a formula linked to interest rates on five-year Treasury notes. Series EE bonds are sold in seven denominations, ranging from $50 to $10,000.

There are no periodic interest payments with EE bonds. Rather, the interest is produced by a gradual increase in the redemption value of a bond over time. When you buy EE bonds, you pay just half the face amount printed on the bond. Thus, the minimum investment is $25.

One other class of savings bonds, designated HH, is also available. Unlike EE bonds, HH bonds pay current interest at a flat rate of 7.5 percent a year. In theory, the EE bonds are designed for accumulation of money, and the HH bonds for use when you want to start drawing current income on that money, say, at retirement.

Before buying savings bonds, an investor should compare their merits with other modern interest-bearing vehicles such as Treasury bonds, notes and bills; money-market funds and money-market deposit accounts; and zero-coupon investments (which operate on an interest-by-appreciation principle similar to that of EE bonds). These may offer higher yields, with equal or only slightly reduced safety, though perhaps not all the tax advantages of savings bonds. Regardless of how you evaluate today's savings bonds, however, most investment experts readily agree that the new ones are an unquestionable improvement over the old ones.

Series EE bonds are not a logical place for money from which you want or need current income. In fact, they are not suited for any funds that you may need to lay your hands on in the near future, since the optimum payoff does not take effect until five years after their issue date.

Series HH bonds, on the other hand, do offer current income. Whether they are desirable for a given investor depends in part on a comparison of their fixed 7.5 percent interest rate against prevailing yields on other, alternative investments. In this comparison, questions of safety and tax advantages should also be taken into account.

Savings bonds are highly liquid, in the sense that you can easily claim your principal and interest after you have held bonds for specified periods of time. But for short periods of time after you buy them, their liquidity is not as good. For example, if you want your money back only a year after buying an EE bond, the floating-rate interest formula does not apply—you receive just 5.5 percent interest on your original investment.

Treasury Bills

When safety is the watchword, many investors the world over think immediately of Treasury bills (T-bills). Like other securities backed by the full faith and credit of the U.S. government, T-bills are regarded as the best credit risk around. Since they have very short lives, Treasury bills involve relatively little market risk in times of volatile interest rates.

T-bills are sold regularly by the Treasury through the 12 regional Federal Reserve banks and the branch offices of those banks. Three-month and six-month bills are auctioned weekly, and 12-month bills every four weeks. They are available in minimum amounts of $10,000 and multiples of $5,000 above that point.

T-bills are the leading investment in the short-term money market. When their prevailing yields rise or fall, returns on other commercial paper tend to move in the same direction. Although large institutions and professional investors play a dominant role in the Treasury bill market, many individual investors buy them directly as well. For people who lack the $10,000 minimum or do not want to take the trouble to invest directly in bills, there is a wide selection of money-market mutual funds that invest only in government securities. Some of these confine themselves strictly to T-bills.

Treasury bills appeal to most investors as a reliable source of generous income, particularly in times when interest rates are high. Like some other types of money-market securities, T-bills do not provide periodic, separate interest payments. Instead, they are sold at a discount from their face value and are subsequently redeemed at full face value. The difference between the purchase and redemption prices constitutes the interest income you receive on your investment.

When you invest in T-bills, you need not worry much about the safety of your money. In recent years, because the government has had to borrow so much, T-bills have provided generous returns. In the future, whenever interest rates or inflation worries are high, T-bills will probably offer attractive returns as well.

They are not, however, the perfect investment for all seasons and purposes. For people with long-term goals, they do not offer the chance to participate in the growth of the economy. Since T-bills are short-term investments, they do not provide a means of locking in a known yield for long periods of time. Furthermore, income-conscious investors who are willing to take a small degree of credit risk can choose among a variety of interest-bearing vehicles that normally carry higher yields than T-bills do.

However, Treasury bills seem likely to retain a unique and valued place in the spectrum of U.S. investments for the foreseeable future. They answer a widespread demand for safety, income, and flexibility in the process of managing money.

With their standing as safe short-term investments, Treasury bills are considered highly liquid. Investors who buy them can choose to tie up their money for as little as three months or less if they buy in the secondary market. In emergencies, T-bills can be sold in the same secondary market before maturity.

Ideally, however, T-bills should be bought with the intention of holding them until they come due, in order to minimize costs that can substantially reduce the return you get from them. Idle cash that may be needed on very short notice can be put instead, at very little increase in risk, in an insured money-market mutual fund that invests solely in government-guaranteed securities like T-bills.

Treasury Bonds and Notes

Treasury bonds and notes may be thought of as longer-lived cousins of Treasury bills. Notes and bonds have many of the same attributes as bills: the safety of the full guarantee of the federal government and its power to collect taxes and regulate the money supply, a fairly generous and assured return, and direct availability at no commission cost from the government. Like Treasury bills in the short-term money market, Treasury bonds and notes are the trend-setting investments in the longer-term credit market.

For all the similarities, government bonds and notes have some significant differences from T-bills. The most obvious is their maturities. Notes may be offered with lives of two to ten years, and bonds from ten-plus years up to nearly 30 years. The longer the maturity, the more exposure a Treasury security has to the risks of inflation and interest rate fluctuations. For this reason, Treasury bonds usually, but not always, offer higher yields than notes, and notes offer higher yields than bills.

Unlike bills, which are sold at discount and redeemed at their face value, notes and bonds pay interest periodically (normally twice a year).

The minimum investment in notes and bonds is lower than for bills. In the cases of notes with maturities of less than four years, it is usually $5,000. With other notes, and with bonds, it is just $1,000. This helps make them a practical possibility for almost all savers and investors.

Because prices of existing Treasury bonds and notes fluctuate constantly with changes in credit conditions, moving in the opposite direction from interest rates, it is very likely that you will realize a capital gain or loss whenever you sell a bond or note before maturity in the secondary market. In times of volatile interest rates, this gain or loss can be considerable.

Like other fixed-income securities, Treasury bonds and notes have important limitations for investors seeking long-term growth through capital appreciation. They cannot grow the way that, say, a stock or real estate investment can.

Treasury bonds and notes generally offer attractive, assured income for savers and investors who want to lock in a given yield for a period of years. People interested in short-term income should investigate buying in the secondary market a note or bond that is nearing maturity and compare what they can earn that way against alternatives like Treasury bills.

Treasury bonds and notes are easy to buy under favorable terms even in small amounts. They offer a wide choice of maturities, and when they come due, you can use them to reinvest your money into new Treasury securities. They are highly marketable, since millions of investors have great faith in the issuer.

However, when you buy notes or bonds, you should be aware that the government does not stand ready to redeem them before maturity. If you want or need to sell a bond or note early, you must turn to a banker or broker for access to the secondary market. Selling this way may involve fees and accepting some price concessions that effectively reduce the return you get on your investment.

Zero-Coupon Investments

Zero-coupon investments (zeros) provide a known return at a set future date on a saver's investment. They serve as an automatic compounding machine. With a conventional bond, the interest rate is known in advance, but its owners have no way of knowing what return they will be able to get in the future when they seek to reinvest the interest payments they receive.

The return available on a zero-coupon investment depends on the prevailing level of interest rates at the time you buy. At a rate of about 11 percent, an initial investment of about $5,000 would grow to $50,000 in about twenty years.

Zeros are available on a variety of interest-bearing investments, including Treasury bonds, municipal bonds, and bank certificates of deposit. Before buying them, investors should consider the safety and stability of both the firm offering them and the issuer of the underlying security. They should also consider their tax circumstances.

Zeros are designed to provide growth in their owners' assets through the compounding of implied interest, in much the same manner as U.S. savings bonds. They are especially well suited for cases in which an investor wants to accumulate a known sum for some anticipated event, such as retirement or a child's entering college.

Zero coupon investments defer the payment of the proceeds until they mature or are sold. Thus, any zeros other than those with very short maturities are unsuitable for investors who want or need maximum current income from their assets.

9

Financial Management
Stretching Dollars

Before retirement, many of us are so busy making money we don't always find the best ways to spend it. After retirement, we have a little more time and find we need to improve our consumer buying skills and begin to save money.

Certain buying strategies can accomplish the following:

- help you get more from your customer dollar without sacrificing quality
- keep you from making needless mistakes
- challenge your current buying patterns

By now, you have verified your actual living expenses in today's dollars and projected those expenses into your retirement. Various buying strategies can help stretch those dollars and allow you to better control some of the expense items highlighted for your desired lifestyle in retirement. Many of these techniques can be used prior to retirement, and all can be used in retirement. Reviewing and updating your expense worksheets every few months on a regular basis will assist you in doing some advanced thinking and planning with respect to your expenditures. This process, combined with dollar-stretching techniques, will help you make better financial decisions.

These techniques apply to all consumer goods and services. They also apply to insurance programs, real estate, and any other major investments. Do not become penny-wise and pound-foolish when applying these techniques, however; quality must never be sacrificed for price. The real purpose is to increase your standard of living, not lower it.

In his book, *Comfort Zones*, Elwood Chapman discussed his dollar-stretching game from which many of the following concepts have been derived.[1]

BUYING TECHNIQUES

Seek Senior Discounts and Create Your Own

You may save more from the technique of discounts than from any other buying strategy. This may be the first time in your life you have group power behind you when it comes to consumer purchases. Senior discounts are legal, and you should be able to build strong relationships with those who offer them.

Senior discounts are common practice in many industries including these:

- airlines
- car rental agencies
- public transportation
- motels and hotels
- beauty shops and barber shops
- retail stores
- amusement parks
- insurance firms
- golf courses
- car repair facilities

Although many discounts are well publicized, you can often negotiate to get better deals.

Get the best possible deal you can before you seek an additional discount. This will prevent retailers from saying they have already given a senior discount when, in effect, they would give the same price break to anyone.

[1]Elwood Chapman, *Comfort Zones* (Los Gatos, CA: Crisp Publications, Inc., 1985)

The way to approach vendors is important. Always do it pleasantly. For example, you might show your AARP (American Association of Retired Persons) card and ask, "Will this make a difference in the price you have quoted?" Your goal is to get the best possible discount and still maintain a good relationship. If you have a chip on your shoulder, it will show, and you may lose more than you gain.

If you are told a senior discount is not provided, you have two choices. Accept the merchandise or service without it or decline pleasantly and look elsewhere. If a discount is granted, thanking the vendor will encourage him or her to treat others as you have been treated.

How much additional money can you save from improving the way you use this technique? It depends on how much time you spend finding those with discount policies for products and services you want and how you go about approaching those who may be willing to provide discounts but do so without a stated policy. It never hurts to ask. Being turned down should not be interpreted as a sign of personal rejection. Think of yourself as a professional buyer who is trained to ask for discounts. If you think of it as a game, you can play and win or stand on the sidelines and lose.

Plan and Buy a Retirement Diet

When professional retail store buyers go to the marketplace, they know what they want to buy before they leave. Often a computer has told them what their customers will likely want: color, style, price, and so on. In other words, they go to market with a specific plan. Once there, they generally stick with their plan.

You should go to your market with similar preparations. If you buy a restricted, quality diet (plan), you should save dollars. This means a carefully prepared list, based on your diet, every time you visit the supermarket. Except for unusual conditions (a party perhaps), no food should be purchased beyond what appears on the diet list. Of course, everyone strays a little, since it is fun to reward ourselves now and then. However, the more you stray from the prepared list, the less you save—and the only thing you gain is weight.

Buy Generic Items

Because of advertising and habit, most people feel safe and comfortable buying name brands. But inflationary pressures, competition, and new marketing techniques have caused changes. Equivalent products are now available at lower prices. The difference is often in the cost of the package itself. The unknown product is usually not in a fancy package, but the product inside is the same. These items are called generic because they are not identified with a well-advertised manufacturer or distributor.

Many pharmacies provide generic (nameless-brand) food supplements and other pharmaceuticals that conform with legal requirements. The prices for these equivalent generic products are usually significantly lower than name brands.

Retail stores, especially large supermarkets, also sell generic items, especially paper goods and packaged food. If you take time to read the labels to ensure you are getting a generic equivalent, you will save money without sacrificing quality. This is possible because packaging, advertising, and distribution expenses have been reduced or eliminated. Stores still make money selling generic items; they just pass some of their savings to you.

Clip and Use Coupons

Name-brand manufacturers send a deluge of coupons into your home through newspapers, magazines, and direct mail. These companies hope you will select their merchandise over that of the competition. Often a store will offer a "double coupons" deal with which you can double your savings.

It is a good buying practice for you to use coupons under the following conditions:

- if it is a food item that fits into your diet plan
- if it is a nonfood item that you actually need or would buy anyway
- if it is a food item, if it's cheaper than an available generic equivalent after the value of the coupon has been deducted
- if you do not have to travel to an out-of-the-way store to redeem the coupon; this can cost you more than you would save

Take Advantage of Sales

Professional buyers look for or wait for deals. A good way for you to find deals on consumer goods is to watch for special sales. Supermarkets often advertise what they call loss leaders. These are advertised items that they sell at a slight loss to attract customers. These are usually good buys, providing you need the merchandise and don't drive too far to get it.

You may save even more when you are ready to purchase big-ticket items. Furniture, appliances, tires, and some clothing fall into this category. Often, it is wise to wait for a sale to get the best price on these items. Stores have traditional sales a few times a year, when they are willing to take substantial markdowns to clean up their inventories.

When buying anything on sale, make sure you follow these three rules:

1. Make certain the merchandise on sale has previously been offered by the same store at a higher price. Some merchants buy special merchandise to offer as sale items, but it has never been sold at a higher price. Stay away from items that say "value $12.85, sale price $7.95." Buy merchandise that says "regular price $12.95, sale price $7.95."

2. Do not fall for the bait-and-switch technique. Some stores advertise an item at a very attractive price (the bait), but when you come in to buy, they discourage the purchase and suggest something higher in price (the switch). This is illegal, but it still happens.

3. Do not buy anything on sale that you would not eventually buy anyway. We sometimes get caught up with sale items and purchase things we never use. When this occurs, our money is wasted.

Follow the Shopping Rule of Three

This means to compare the prices of identical or similar items of equal quality using three different sources.

Let's assume you need tires for your car. The rule says that you should check with three different outlets to get prices on the same-quality tire. It is always a good policy to inform each store that you are shopping at other suppliers and will eventually take the best price consistent with quality. Once you narrow your choice, ask if the tires you intend to buy will be on sale in the near future. This could turn out to be a double savings. Finally, you ask if a senior discount might also apply.

Keep in mind that certain items almost always are on sale by merchants. Tires and shock absorbers fall into this category. Also, household appliances, shoes, clothing, and many other items are regularly on sale. Apply the rule of three on any item selling above $50.

Here are some other shopping tips to remember:

- Compare a traditional retailer (department store) with a discount house (K-Mart, Best) to get a marketwide comparison. Discount houses frequently offer fewer services in a less-posh setting but have lower prices on identical items.

- Don't neglect catalogs. One way to do this is to find the exact merchandise you want on the retailer's floor and then check the catalog to see if you can order it at a lower price.
- Make certain the item you eventually choose is the same as or better than those offered by others. It is a mistake to shop and then settle for something of less quality. Remember the expression, "Quality is remembered long after price is forgotten."

Make Favorable Contracts

Professional buyers sign purchase orders when they buy from vendors. These documents deal with specifics of the purchase and guarantee the rights of both parties. In a sense, you do the same whenever you agree to have repairs done on your automobile, home, or other possessions.

Assume you need to have your automobile tuned. In this case, you might shop by telephone (using the rule of three) before deciding on a certain garage. If the prices are close, you may feel most comfortable with your regular mechanic. You should, however, get a fixed estimate for the work to be done. Ask the necessary questions to ensure you are getting the service you desire. Sign a work order only after making sure it conforms to the conditions desired and agreed upon. At this point, the mechanic should be told that if any additional work is needed, you personally must authorize the work. Should you receive a call, for example, informing you that new brakes are required or you have a major problem with your clutch or transmission, feel free to return to the rule of three and get other opinions. If your mechanic resists, it could be a signal you are paying for unnecessary repairs.

Contracts require good communication; don't let anyone rush you. The goal is for you to be satisfied and for the contractor to make a reasonable profit. Try to make the agreements mutually rewarding. This is especially true when you work with painters, interior designers, and those who do home repairs. To accomplish this, you must stay in charge.

Both small contracting jobs (having your television repaired) or big jobs (installing a new roof) can present problems if the specifics are not discussed in advance. Questions should be asked before, not after. It is much better to get a good contract initially than to be forced to create one later to correct misunderstandings.

It is a good policy never to pay a bill until you are fully satisfied. If a painting job has been done in your home, carefully inspect the work before you pay the bill. This way the contractor will return to make corrections and get paid.

Avoid Major Rip-offs

Everyone is vulnerable to con artists now and then. What can you do to protect yourself?

* Be aware that there are unethical individuals who will try to trick you into something you do not want or should buy from another source.
* Consult a qualified second party before signing anything that is not routine.
* Do not sign until you have done some research and verification. Remember to use the rule of three.

Demand Satisfaction

If you purchase a product in good faith and it does not live up to your expectations, return it no matter how much time has elapsed. This is true whether or not you have a warranty or guarantee. Most retailers stand behind what they sell. They want to protect their relationship with you and your friends.

Many people hesitate to return merchandise. Some are not familiar with laws protecting consumers' rights. Others anticipate a hassle or an embarrassing scene and are reluctant to inquire. They would rather keep inferior merchandise than make the effort to exchange it.

Buy Only What You Need or Will Use

A fashion buyer for a retail store knows that if she selects dresses her customers won't buy because of fashion or price, she will have to reduce the price drastically to get rid of them. If you buy clothing and hang it in your closet without wearing it, you also have lost money.

The idea is to spend your discretionary funds to enrich your life. If you buy something you don't need, you are denying yourself something you could enjoy. Like most people, you probably have too much tucked away in closets or drawers gathering dust.

One way to avoid making unnecessary purchases is to keep asking questions such as these:

* Am I buying this for myself or for my heirs?
* Do I really need it?
* Will I really use it?
* Would I rather add to my possessions or increase the fun I could have?
* Do I already have enough of what I am about to buy?

Shop by Telephone

It is amazing how much time (your most precious commodity) you can conserve and how much money you can save by shopping and collecting information on the telephone. You can easily apply the rule of three by telephone. If you don't have time to visit three stores personally, you can always call and compare prices.

Other ways to use the telephone to save money include these:

- Verify that a store has the item you seek before you go there.
- Ask whether a sale is pending so you can decide to delay a purchase and save.
- Learn ahead of time if the store has a senior discount program or policy.

Negotiate

Most people do not like to bargain for a price. They accept prices or conditions to avoid a hassle. Professional buyers, on the other hand, learn to negotiate and enjoy it. They earn more respect from customers and their employers when they negotiate well. The same is true for you. Vendors will respect you more when you learn to negotiate properly.

Here are some conditions under which you should consider negotiating:

- When you sense the quoted price is flexible, and others may be getting a lower price than you.
- When the seller invites you to make an offer. Sometimes this is stated openly; at other times it is implied.
- When it is a buyer's market. For example: When automobiles, homes, and similar products are not selling well and you know it.

A gentle way to discover if negotiation is possible is the simple question, "May I make an offer or are your prices firm?" If you get a "no" answer, you know where you stand. If negotiation is welcome, you should make sure that your offer is realistically low so there is room for additional negotiation by both parties.

If you feel uncomfortable negotiating, take someone along who enjoys it. This person will feel good about helping you get a better price on something, and probably will appreciate being asked.

Work with Other People's Money

Purchasing agents learn to use the money of the seller rather than that of their own firm. For example, they delay payment of bills up to the contractual limit to keep their money earning interest. If you use credit cards (MasterCard, Visa, and so on) and delay making your payment until toward the due date of the statement, you are following this principle. You might take a trip and charge $2,000 on your credit card. The bill arrives after your return, and you pay it early the week it is due. Good! You have used their money on the trip.

Here are some other ways to work with the money of others:

- When making contracts to get work done, make it clear that payment is due only after the work is completed.
- Use the maximum time for noninterest payment permitted by sellers (usually shown on your statement).
- Don't pay a bill until a few days before it is due.
- Keep your money in a place that will draw interest for you.

Take Advantage of Off-Season Opportunities

When it comes to vacations, retirees often have more choice than those who work. Not only is it less expensive to visit a resort area during the off-season, but also there are fewer people to contend with in restaurants and while sightseeing. This is especially true in Hawaii, Mexico, and Florida, where the climate is temperate year-round. Off-season savings usually apply to hotel and motel accommodations, air fares, and rental cars, as well as meals and services. Savings are substantial.

Epilogue

Whatever your age, it is never too soon to look ahead and begin giving thought to your retirement. When the time finally comes, the transition will be smooth, and you will feel comfortable and secure about it.

Today, more than ever, as the society we live in becomes more demanding, planning for retirement is a necessity. You must plan ahead by setting goals and deciding how they will be met. Retirement planning also means getting ready for a lifestyle change as well as a changing financial picture.

You may be faced with some hard choices. You may find yourself staring at lobster tails, wishing you could afford some. You may find yourself having to choose whether to put your spouse—the man or woman with whom you've spent the last 50 years—into a no-frills nursing home or a nursing home with big bay windows, a view of the ocean, and a private sitter. You may find yourself hovering between poverty and comfort. And you may find yourself considering just how much or how little you want to leave your children. These are all difficult decisions that might be made easier if the proper planning is done ahead of time.

But whatever your goals may be, plan ahead for your retirement as a renewal and a beginning, one that opens up a world of possibilities and opportunities.

Useful Resources

MEMBERSHIP ORGANIZATIONS

American Association of
Retired Persons (AARP)
1909 K Street, N.W.
Washington, DC 20049
(202) 872-4700

Action for Independent
Maturity (AIM)
1909 K Street, N.W.
Washington, DC 20049
(202) 872-4850

Institute of Lifetime Learning
1346 Connecticut Avenue, N.W.
Washington, DC 20036
or
215 Long Beach Boulevard
Long Beach, CA 90802

National Retired Teachers
Association (NRTA)
1909 K Street, N.W.
Washington, DC 20049
(202) 872-4700

Gray Panthers
3700 Chestnut Street
Philadelphia, PA 19104

EDUCATION

Adult Education Association
  of the U.S.A.
810 18th Street, N.W.
Washington, DC 20006

National Association for Public
  Continuing and Adult
  Education
1201 16th Street, N.W.
Washington, DC 20036

U.S. Department of Education
Bureau of Adult, Vocational
  and Library Programs
Seventh & D Streets, S.W.
Washington, DC 20202

Institute of Lifetime
  Learning
1909 K Street, N.W.
Washington, DC 20006

National Home Study
  Council
1601 18th Street, N.W.
Washington, DC 20009

HEALTH

Alzheimer's Disease and Related
  Disorders Association, Inc.
360 N. Michigan Avenue
Chicago, IL 60601

American Cancer Society, Inc.
777 Third Avenue
New York, NY 10017

American Dietetic Association
430 N. Michigan Avenue
Chicago, IL 60611

American Heart Association
44 East 23rd Street
New York, NY 10010

American Optometric
  Association
7000 Chippewa Street
St. Louis, MO 63119

American Speech and Hearing
  Association
9030 Old Georgetown Road,
  N.W.
Washington, DC 20014

National Association of Jewish
  Homes for the Aged
2525 Centerville Road
Dallas, TX 75228

American Association of
  Homes for the Aging
1050 17th Street, N.W.
Washington, DC 20036

American Dental Association
211 E. Chicago Avenue
Chicago, IL 60611

American Foundation for the
  Blind
15 W. 16th Street
New York, NY 10011

American Health Care
  Association
1200 15th Street, N.W.
Washington, DC 20005

American Podiatry Association
20 Chevy Chase Circle, N.W.
Washington, DC 20015

Arthritis Foundation
221 Park Avenue South
New York, NY 10003

National Cancer Institute
Office of Cancer
  Communications
Bethesda, MD 20205

LEGAL SERVICES

American Bar Association
1155 East 60th Street
Chicago, IL 60637

National Senior Citizens Law
  Center
1709 W. Eighth Street
Los Angeles, CA 90017

National Legal Aid and
  Defenders Association
2100 M Street, N.W.
Washington, DC 20037

PAID EMPLOYMENT

Green Thumb, Inc.
1012 14th Street, N.W.
Washington, DC 20005

National Council of Senior
  Citizens
1511 K Street, N.W.
Washington, DC 20036

U.S. Small Business
  Administration
1441 L Street, N.W.
Washington, DC 20549

Mature Temps
Exxon Building
1251 Avenue of the Americas
New York, NY 10020

National Council on the Aging
1828 L Street, N.W.
Washington, DC 20036

TRAVEL

BritRail Travel International,
  Inc.
630 Third Avenue
New York, NY 10017

EurailPass
  c/o French National Railroad
610 Fifth Avenue
New York, NY 10020

Floating Through Europe
271 Madison Avenue
New York, NY 10016

Elderhostel
80 Boylston Street
Suite #400
Boston, MA 02116

Farm and Ranch Vacations
36 East 57th Street
New York, NY 10022

U.S. Department of Interior
   National Park Service
18th and C Streets, N.W.
Washington, DC 20240

VOLUNTEER WORK

Action
806 Connecticut Avenue, N.W.
Washington, DC 20525
(202) 393-3111

INFORMATION ON INSURANCE

American Association of Retired
   Persons (AARP)
1909 K Street, N.W.
Washington, DC 20049

Write for their offerings on the
   insurance field.

Consumer Information Center
Pueblo, CO 81009

Write for their free catalog of
   government publications.

Department of Health and
   Human Services
Health Care Financing
   Administration
Baltimore, MD 21207

Write for their free booklet
   *Guide to Health Insurance for
   People with Medicare* and for
   a list of other booklets and
   pamphlets.

National Institute on Aging
Information Office
90 Rockville Pike
Bethesda, MD 20205

Offers information on insurance
   and health care.

Insurance Information Institute
110 William Street
New York, NY 10038

Offers information on
   homeowner's insurance.

American Council of Life
   Insurance
1850 K Street, N.W.
Washington, DC 20006

Offers information on life
   insurance, health insurance,
   pensions, and other related
   data.

INFORMATION ON HMOs

Office of Health Maintenance
   Organizations
Park Building, Room 310
12420 Parklawn Drive
Rockville, MD 20857

Group Health Association of
   America, Inc.
624 9th Street, N.W., Suite 700
Washington, DC 20001

Index